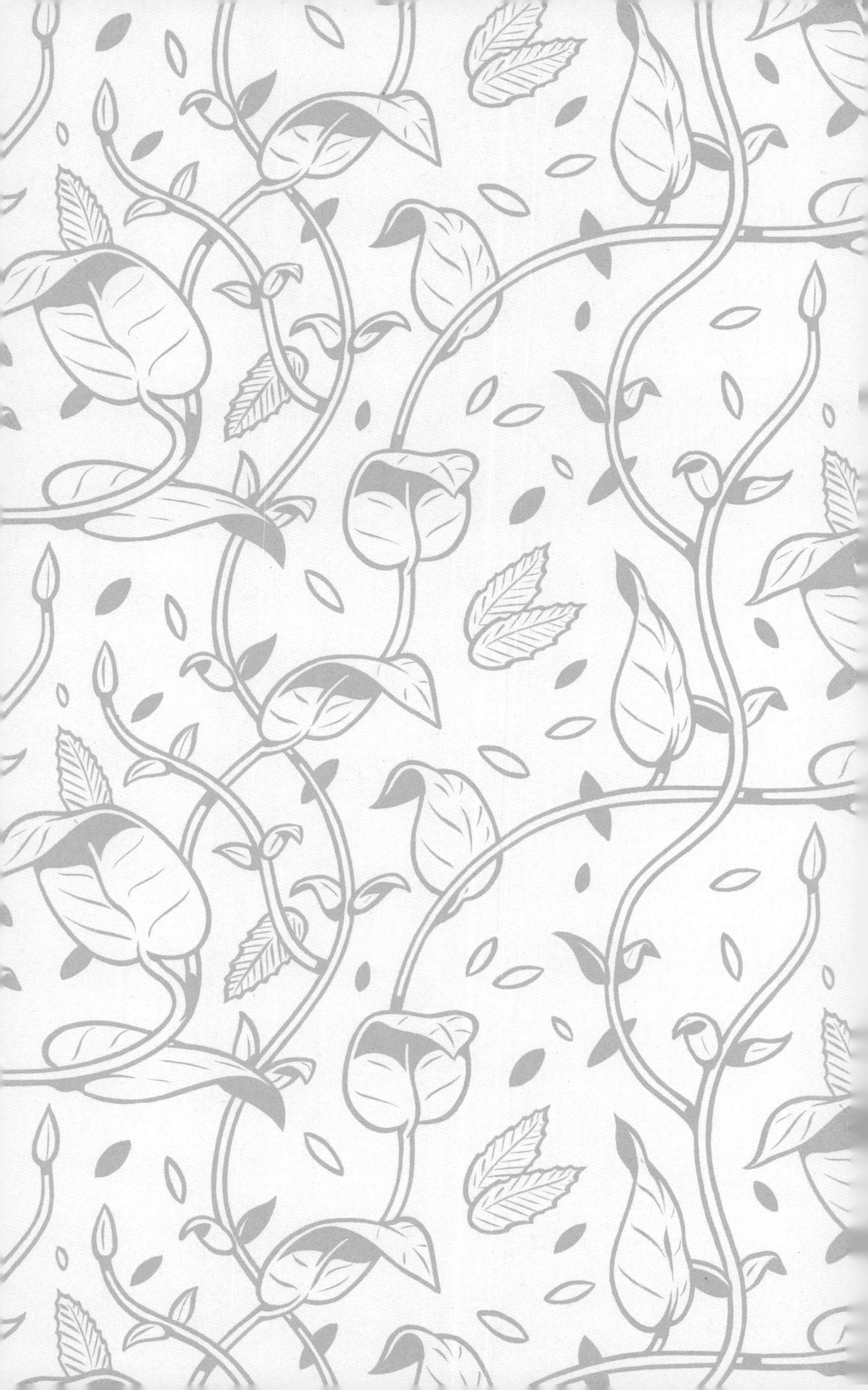

THE DEADLIEST FLOWER

Eleanor
Spicer Rice

illustrated by
Max Temescu

Norton Young Readers
An Imprint of W. W. Norton & Company
Independent Publishers Since 1923

For Jane SF, who knows about flowers —E.S.R.
For Aunt Helen —M.T.

Text copyright © 2025 by Eleanor Spicer Rice
Illustrations copyright © 2025 by Max Temescu

All rights reserved
Printed in Canada
First Edition

For information about permission to reproduce selections from this book, write to
Permissions, W. W. Norton & Company, Inc., 500 Fifth Avenue, New York, NY 10110

For information about special discounts for bulk purchases, please contact
W. W. Norton Special Sales at specialsales@wwnorton.com or 800-233-4830

Manufacturing by Marquis
Book design by Hana Anouk Nakamura
Production manager: Delaney Adams

ISBN 978-1-324-05377-4

W. W. Norton & Company, Inc., 500 Fifth Avenue, New York, NY 10110
www.wwnorton.com

W. W. Norton & Company Ltd., 15 Carlisle Street, London W1D 3BS

1 2 3 4 5 6 7 8 9 0

WARNING!

YOU ARE ABOUT TO SEE SOME OF THE DEADLIEST FLOWERING PLANTS ON EARTH. SOME BLOOM FAR AWAY FROM YOU. OTHERS MAY SPROUT IN YOUR LAWN THIS SPRING.

Two good rules for all wild plants, deadly or not:

1. Do not eat them. No blossom salads, leaf sandwiches, random berry ice cream, stick pizzas. You have lots of vegetables you already complain about eating! Why add more greens to your life?!

R.I.P.
KILLED BY BROCCOLI'S GROSSNESS

2. Do not pick them. Some plants are so toxic their poisons can seep through your skin just by holding their stems. If you don't know what it is, don't pick it! Leave it for the birds! Also, learn what plants are around you! They're amazing!

these pages, you'll meet six types of plants that hide deadly poison behind eir pretty blooms. Which beautiful blossom will be crowned **THE DEADLIEST**?

WHO WILL IT BE? THE BEAUTIFUL LADY BELLADONNA? THE HEAVENLY-SEEMING ANGEL'S TRUMPET? OR SOMEONE ELSE? LET'S FIND OUT!

THIS IS A FLOWERING PLANT

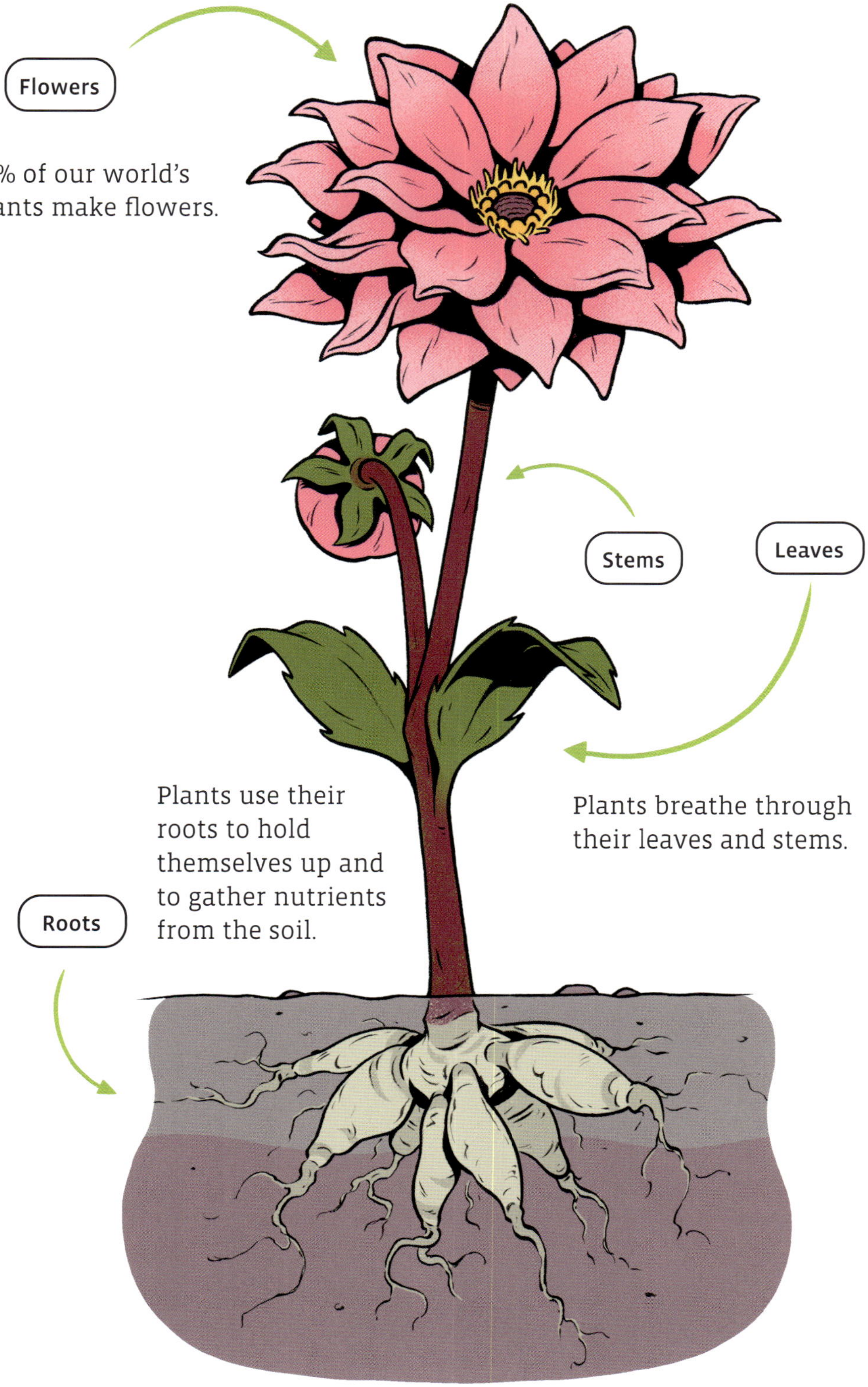
Flowers
90% of our world's plants make flowers.
Stems
Leaves
Plants breathe through their leaves and stems.
Plants use their roots to hold themselves up and to gather nutrients from the soil.
Roots

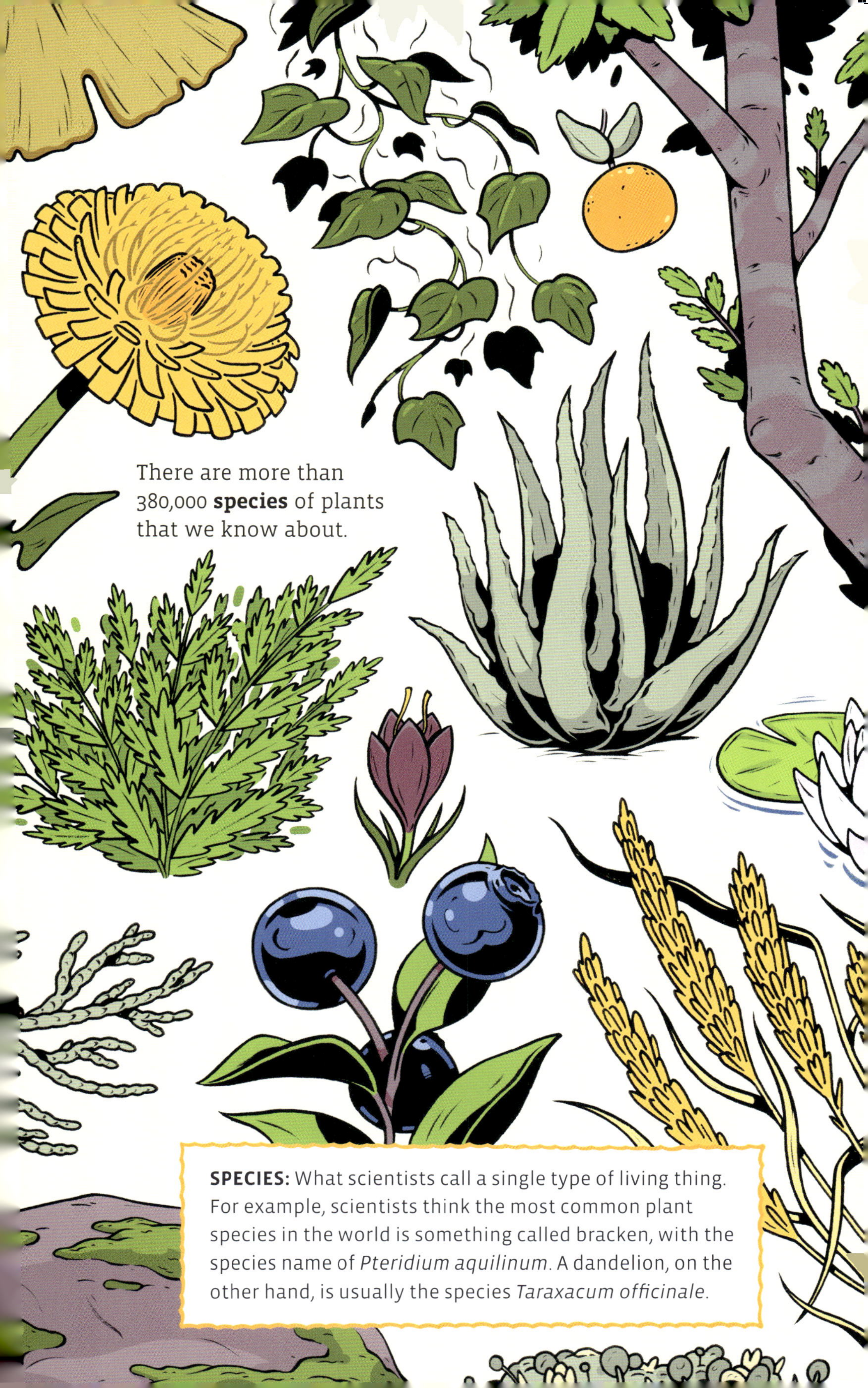

There are more than 380,000 **species** of plants that we know about.

SPECIES: What scientists call a single type of living thing. For example, scientists think the most common plant species in the world is something called bracken, with the species name of *Pteridium aquilinum*. A dandelion, on the other hand, is usually the species *Taraxacum officinale*.

WHY ARE SOME PLANTS SUPER DEADLY?

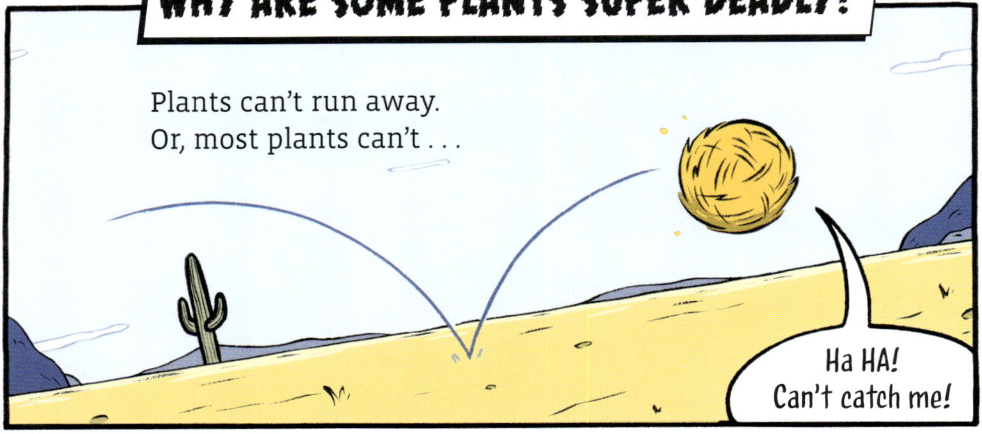

Plants can't run away.
Or, most plants can't . . .
Ha HA! Can't catch me!

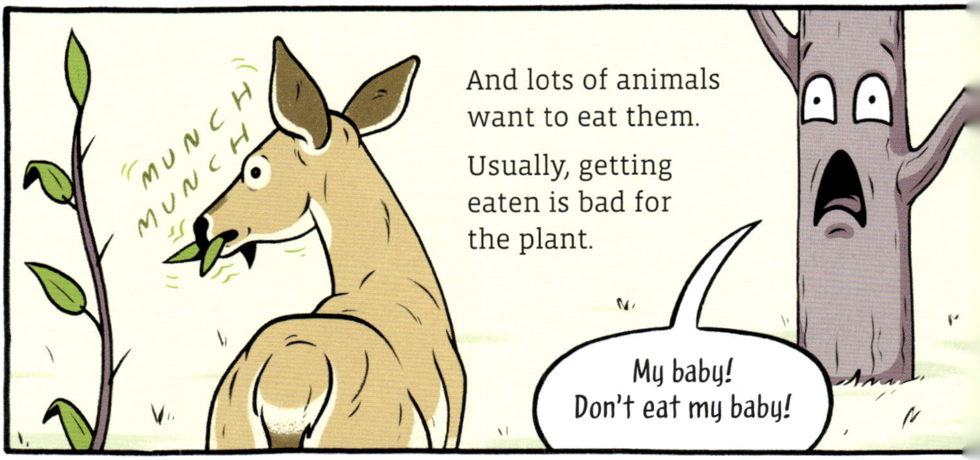

MUNCH MUNCH
And lots of animals want to eat them.
Usually, getting eaten is bad for the plant.
My baby! Don't eat my baby!

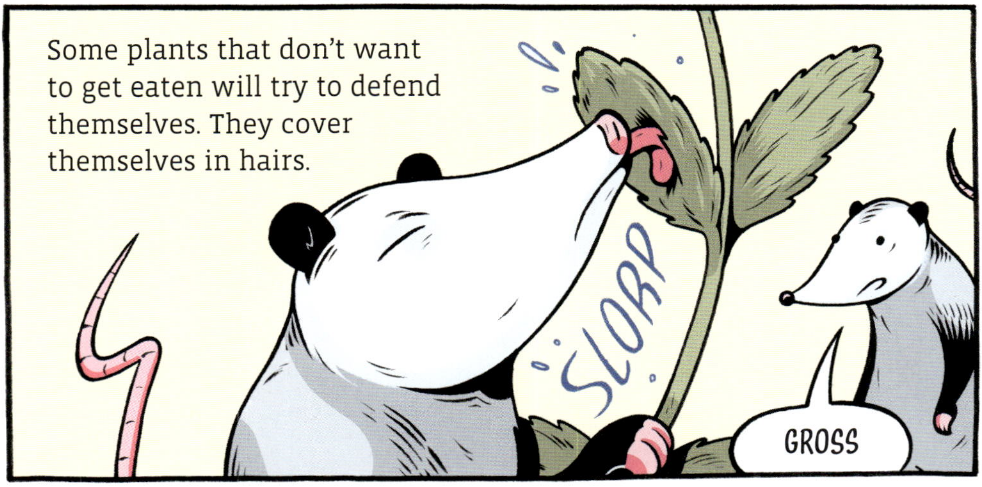

Some plants that don't want to get eaten will try to defend themselves. They cover themselves in hairs.
SLORP
GROSS

Or thorns . . .

Or sticky stuff . . .

Or they defend themselves by tasting bad or making the animals that eat them sick. The stuff that tastes bad or can make us sick are a plant's **toxins**.

TOXIN: a chemical that living things make that make you sick or kill you

WHY DON'T WE JUST GET RID OF ALL THE TOXIC PLANTS?

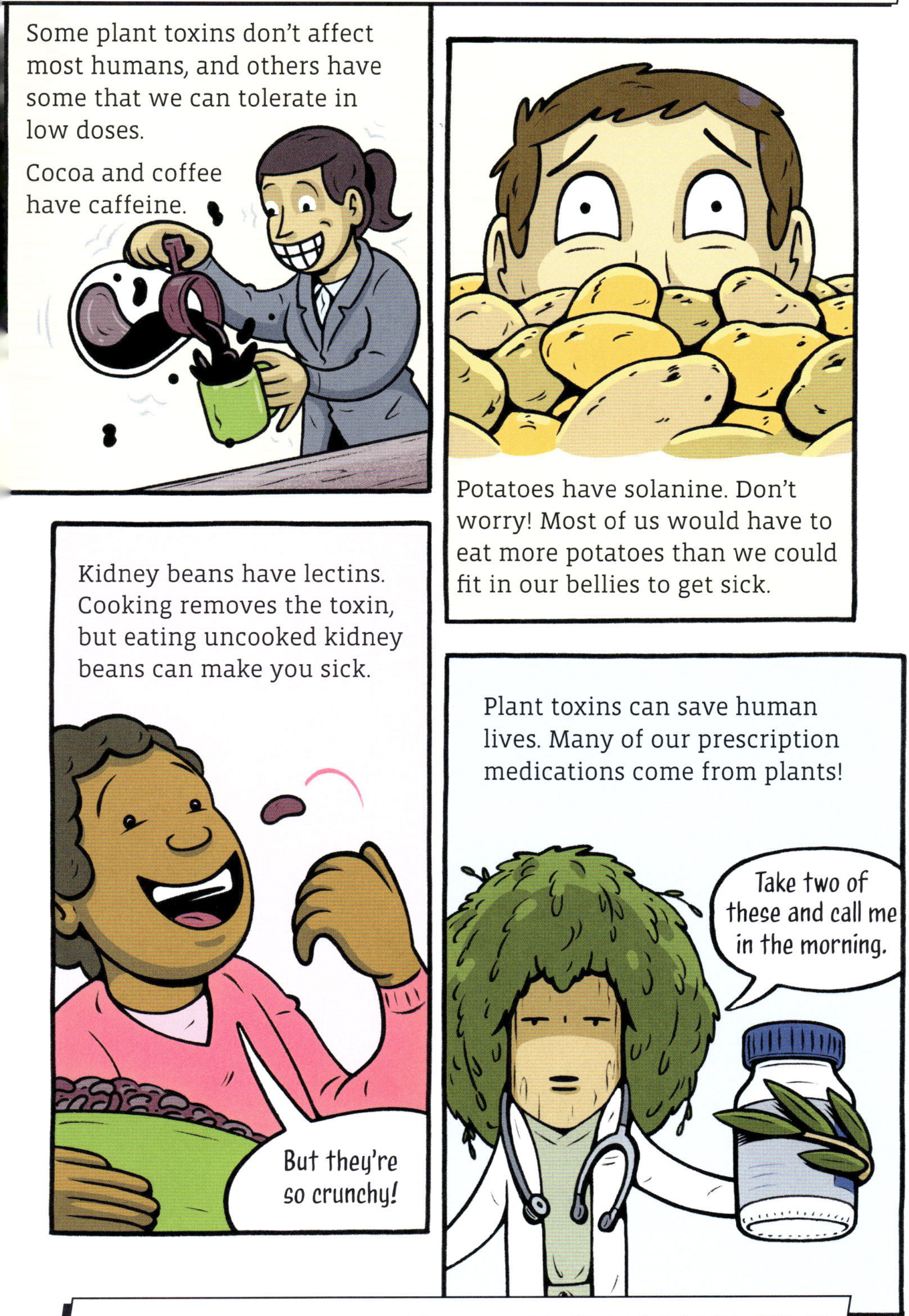
Some plant toxins don't affect most humans, and others have some that we can tolerate in low doses.
Cocoa and coffee have caffeine.
Potatoes have solanine. Don't worry! Most of us would have to eat more potatoes than we could fit in our bellies to get sick.
Kidney beans have lectins. Cooking removes the toxin, but eating uncooked kidney beans can make you sick.
But they're so crunchy!
Plant toxins can save human lives. Many of our prescription medications come from plants!
Take two of these and call me in the morning.

WE HAVE TOXIC PLANTS. WE NEED THEM! LET'S LOVE THEM!

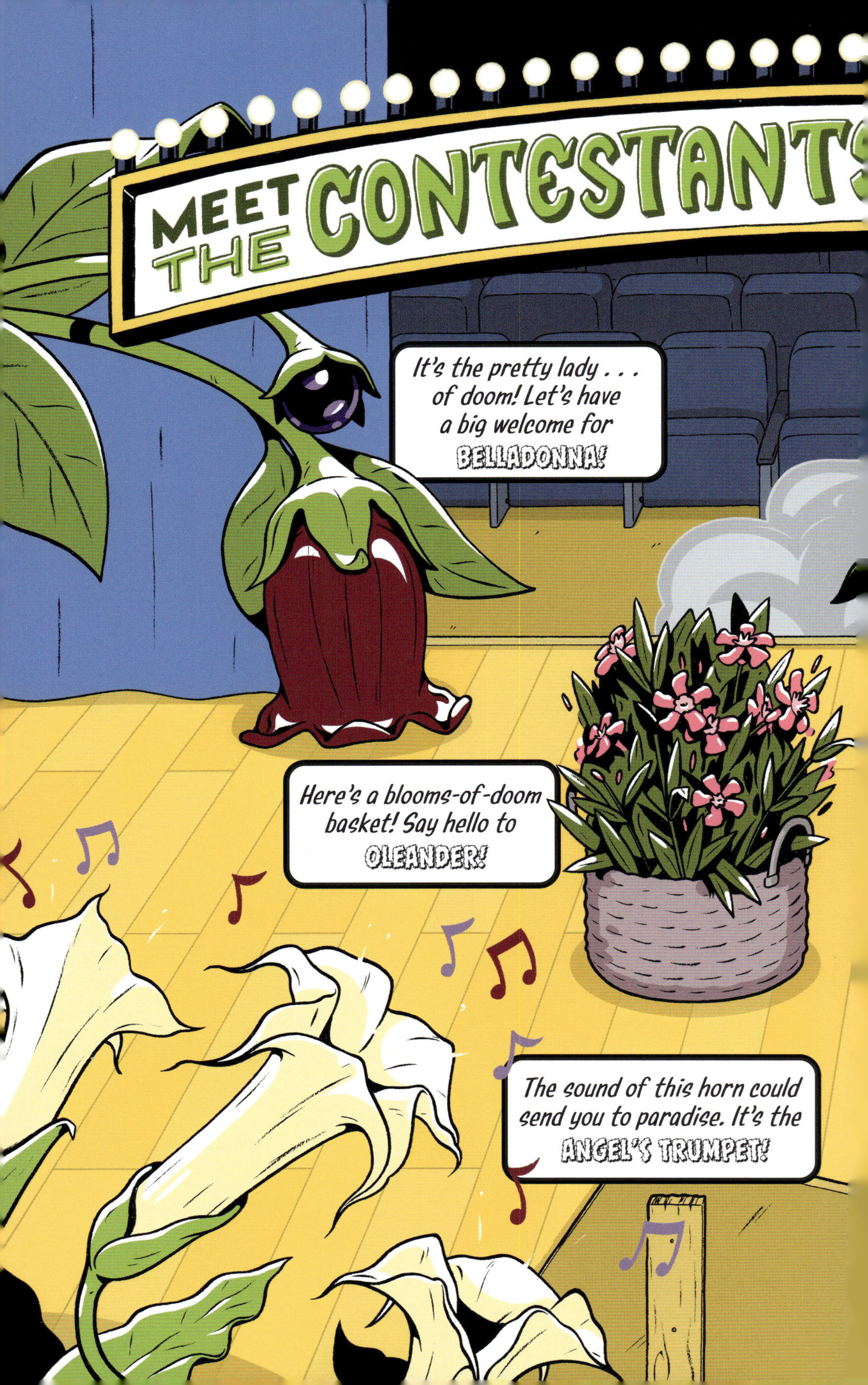
MEET THE CONTESTANTS
It's the pretty lady . . . of doom! Let's have a big welcome for BELLADONNA!
Here's a blooms-of-doom basket! Say hello to OLEANDER!
The sound of this horn could send you to paradise. It's the ANGEL'S TRUMPET!

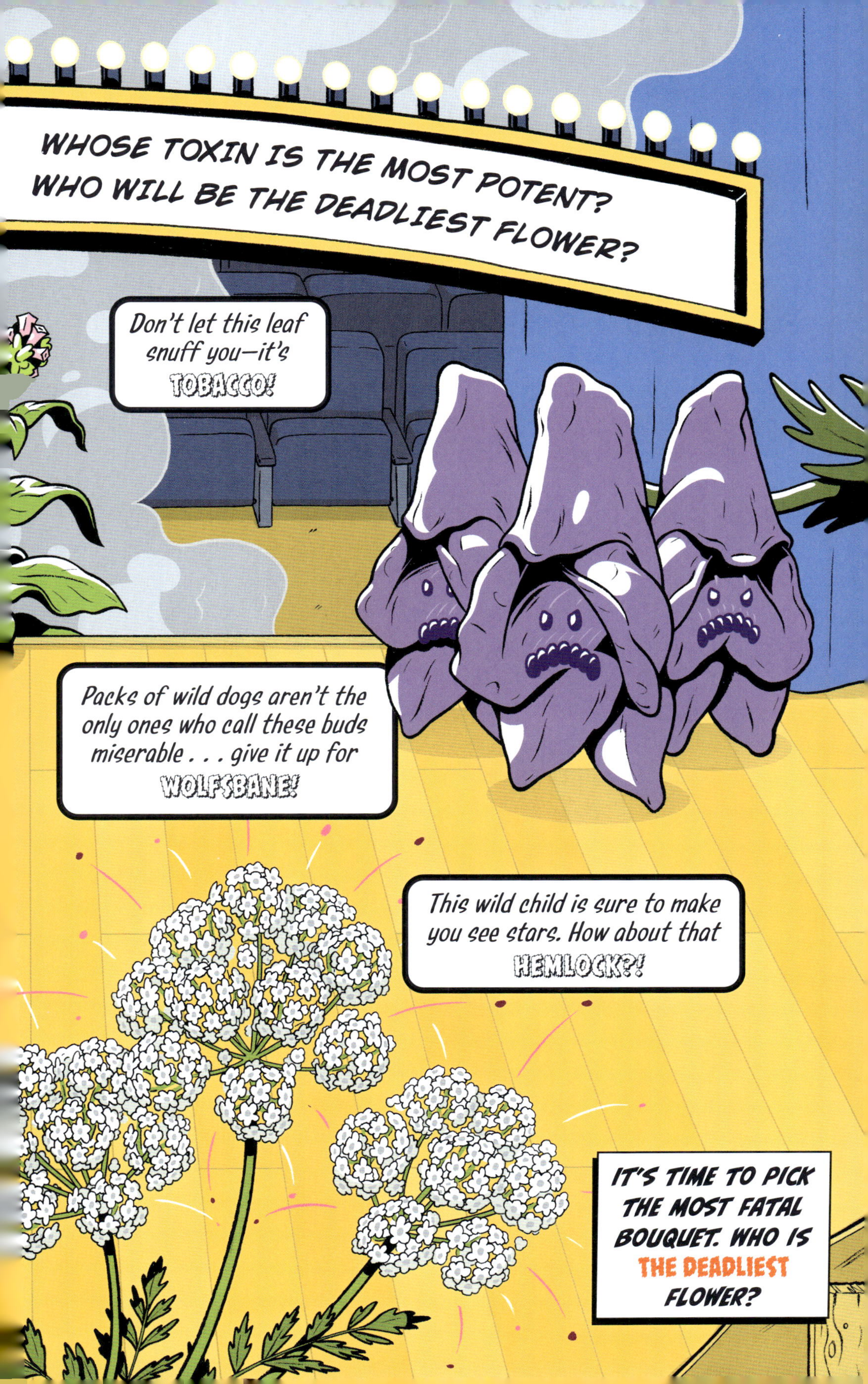

WHOSE TOXIN IS THE MOST POTENT? WHO WILL BE THE DEADLIEST FLOWER?
Don't let this leaf snuff you—it's TOBACCO!
Packs of wild dogs aren't the only ones who call these buds miserable . . . give it up for WOLFSBANE!
This wild child is sure to make you see stars. How about that HEMLOCK?!
IT'S TIME TO PICK THE MOST FATAL BOUQUET. WHO IS THE DEADLIEST FLOWER?

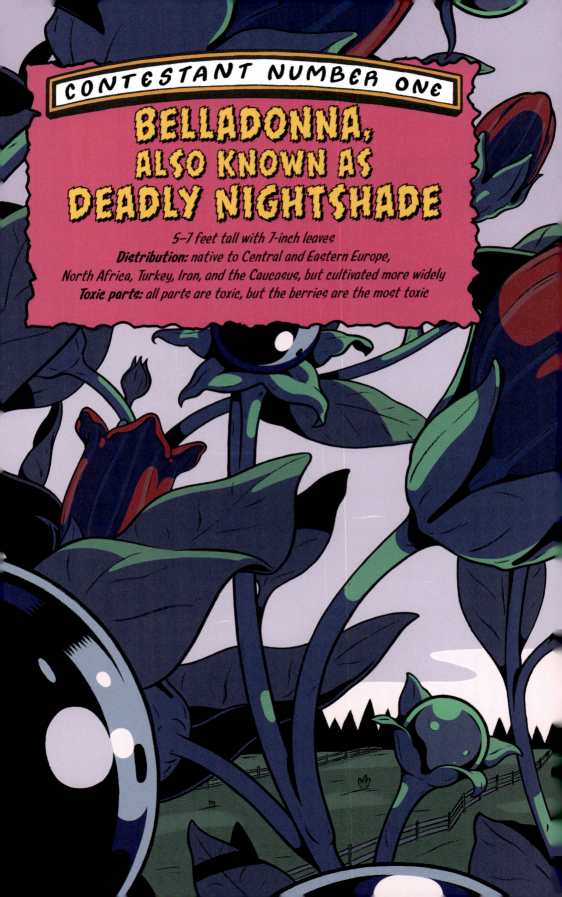

CONTESTANT NUMBER ONE

BELLADONNA, ALSO KNOWN AS DEADLY NIGHTSHADE

5–7 feet tall with 7-inch leaves

Distribution: native to Central and Eastern Europe, North Africa, Turkey, Iran, and the Caucasus, but cultivated more widely

Toxic parts: all parts are toxic, but the berries are the most toxic

Deadly nightshade's scientific name is *Atropos belladonna.*

Atropos is one of the three fates of Greek mythology. She cut the thread of life.

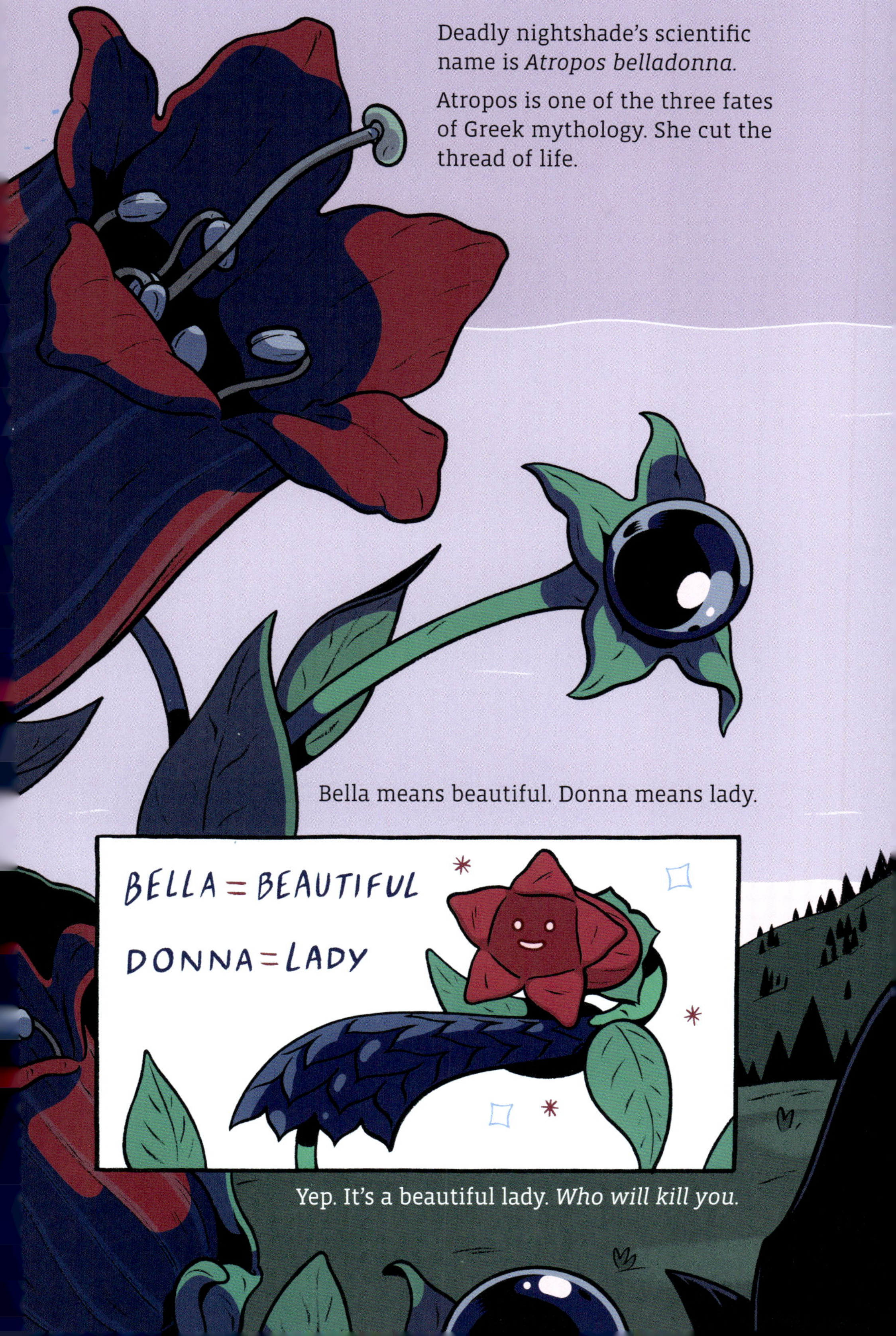
BELLA = BEAUTIFUL
DONNA = LADY

Bella means beautiful. Donna means lady.

Yep. It's a beautiful lady. *Who will kill you.*

In the Middle Ages, women used to put belladonna drops in their eyes to make them big and beautiful.

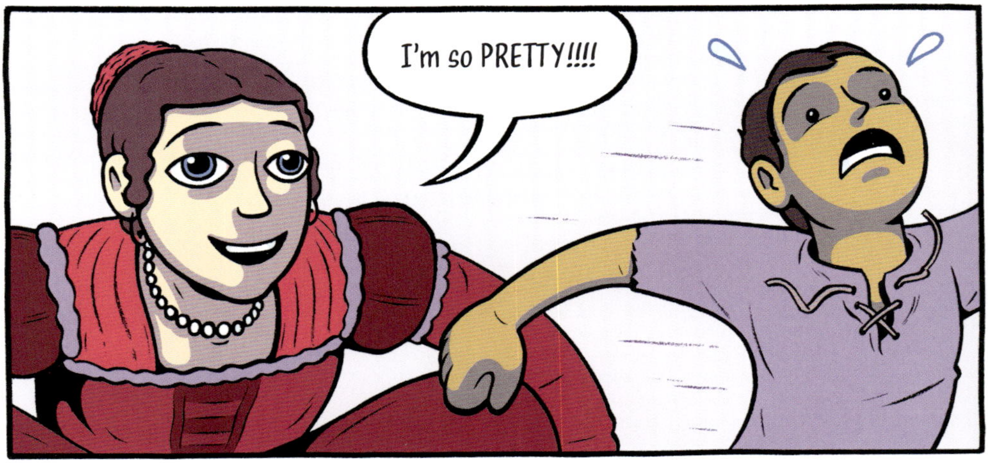
I'm so PRETTY!!!!

They knew that eating nightshade could kill them. They also knew that putting drops of nightshade in their eyes made their **pupils dilate**.

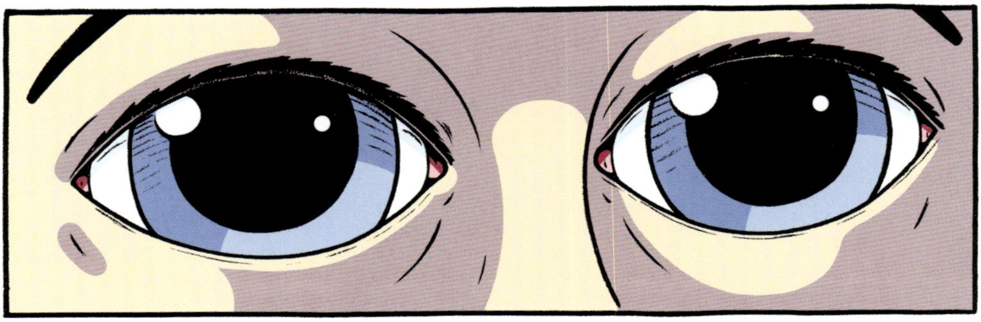

That's . . . nice? But what else can it do?

Well, people have used nightshade to kill other people for hundreds of years.

The ancient Romans dipped their spears and arrows in nightshade paste.

People used nightshade **tinctures** to poison emperors, kings, and just regular folks they wanted out of the way.

PUPIL: the black part of your eye. To **DILATE** something means to make it bigger.

TINCTURE: a drug dissolved in alcohol.

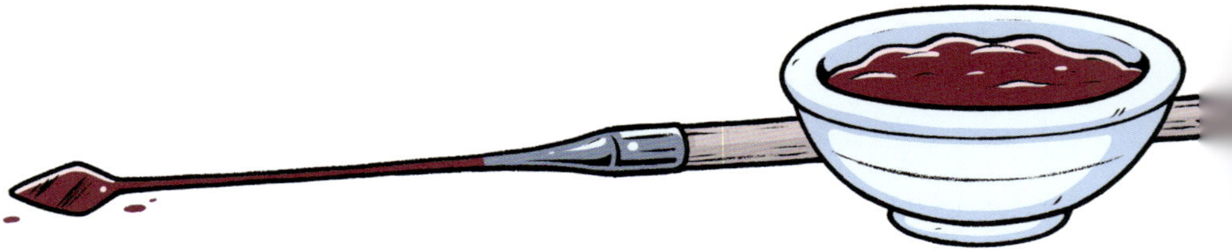

WHAT IF SOMEONE WANTED YOU OUT OF THE WAY? WHAT IF YOU DRANK BELLADONNA TEA?

About an hour after you drink it, your body temperature will skyrocket.

Six to eight hours later, your pupils will dilate. You'll stop being able to see too well.

Your veins will expand. Your face will flush.

u will start to slur your words.

ur mouth and throat will become ry dry.

u will lose the ability to walk. You ill become confused and unaware your surroundings.

You could **hallucinate**.

Your body will start to **convulse**.

You will not be able to breathe. You will slip into unconsciousness and die.

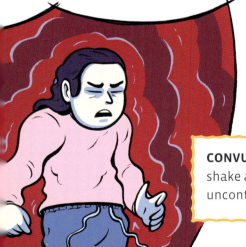

HALLUCINATE: to see something that's not actually there.

CONVULSE: to shake and tremor uncontrollably.

THAT'S PRETTY DEADLY! BUT IS IT THE DEADLIEST?

CONTESTANT NUMBER TWO

OLEANDER

Shrub or small tree, 7–20 feet tall
Distribution: *temperate, subtropical, and tropical climates worldwide*
Toxic parts: *all parts are toxic*

Poisons flow through every part of the oleander plant. Many consider it a bouquet of dismay. But some think of it as a helpful hero.

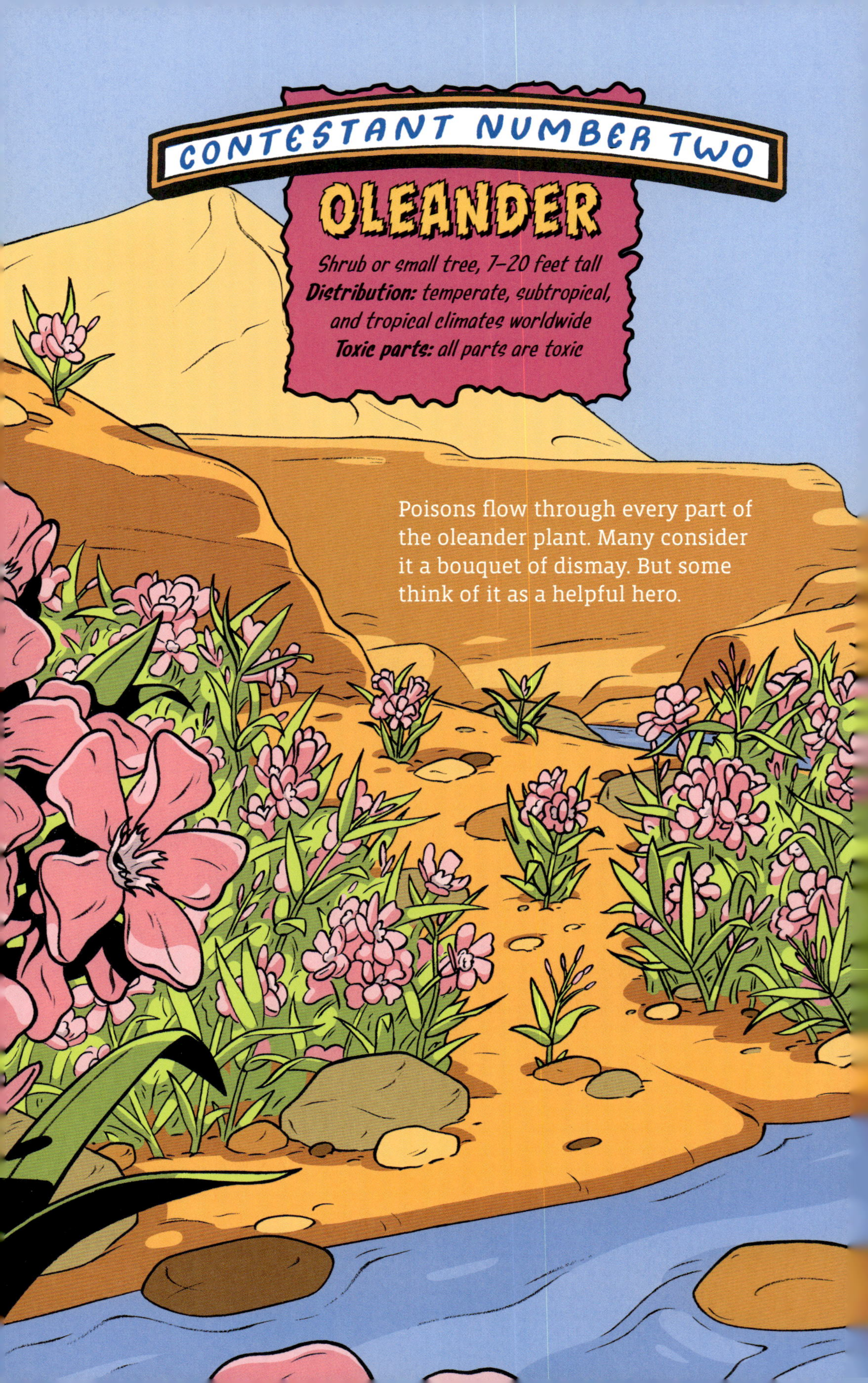

A few caterpillar species can eat its leaves without coming to any harm. They can even store up oleander toxins to give a deadly surprise to anyone who might enjoy snacking on caterpillars.

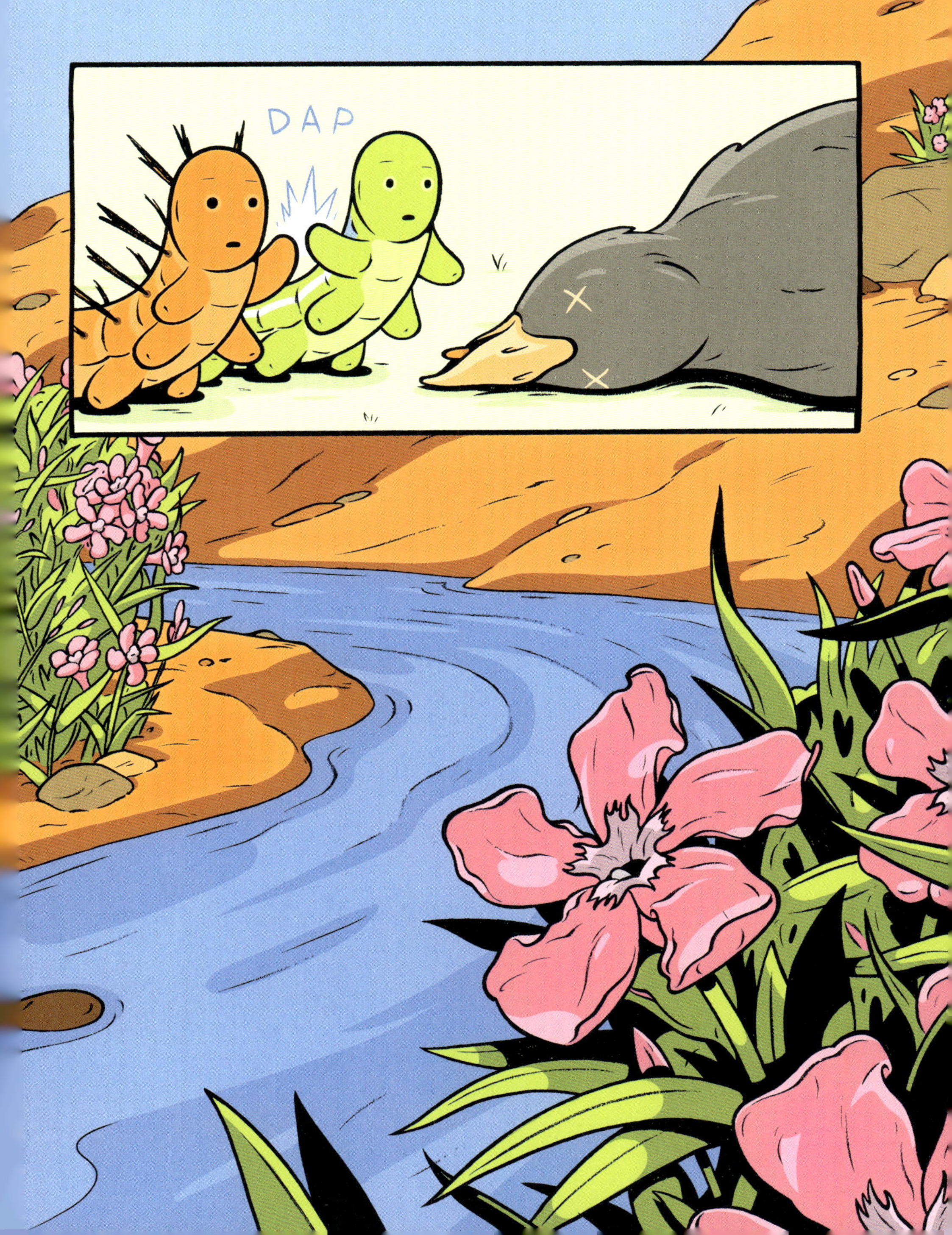
DAP

It didn't take humans long to figure out how oleander could help them, too.

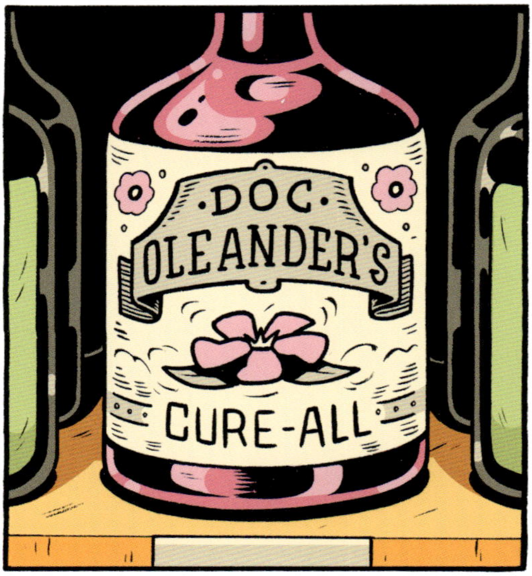
DOC
OLEANDER'S
CURE-ALL

For centuries, people have mashed oleander into a pulp and rubbed it on their bodies to treat everything from snake bites to body lice.

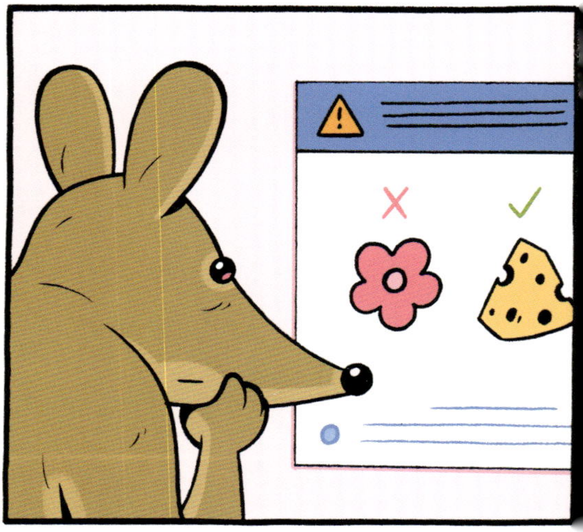

They used oleander to poison rats and mice stealing people's food.

And occasionally brewed it into deadly teas to kill their enemies.

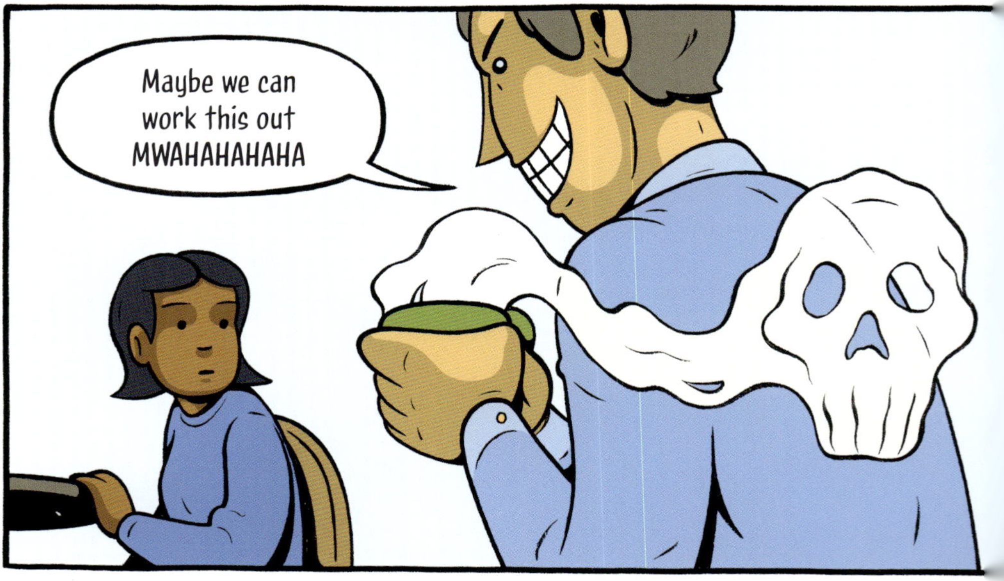
Maybe we can work this out MWAHAHAHAHA

WHAT IF SOMEONE GAVE YOU AN OLEANDER SANDWICH?

Well, first, don't make enemies. Life is too short for that. Make friends! Ignore the mean and evil people.

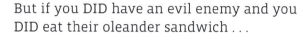

But if you DID have an evil enemy and you DID eat their oleander sandwich . . .

. . . about four hours after your Catastrophe on Rye, you'll start to feel sick to your stomach.

You will feel nauseous, begin to vomit, and have diarrhea as your body tries to get the poison out of its system.

It's no use. You won't realize the awful horridness coming.

You won't realize that oleander's toxins attack your heart.

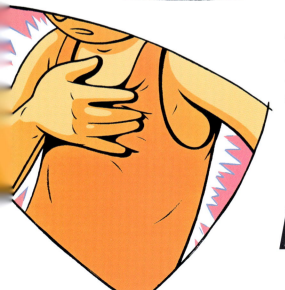

Your heart will start to beat out of rhythm. You will have a heart attack. You'll never eat another sandwich again.

THAT'S ONE DEADLY DOSE. BUT IS IT THE DEADLIEST?

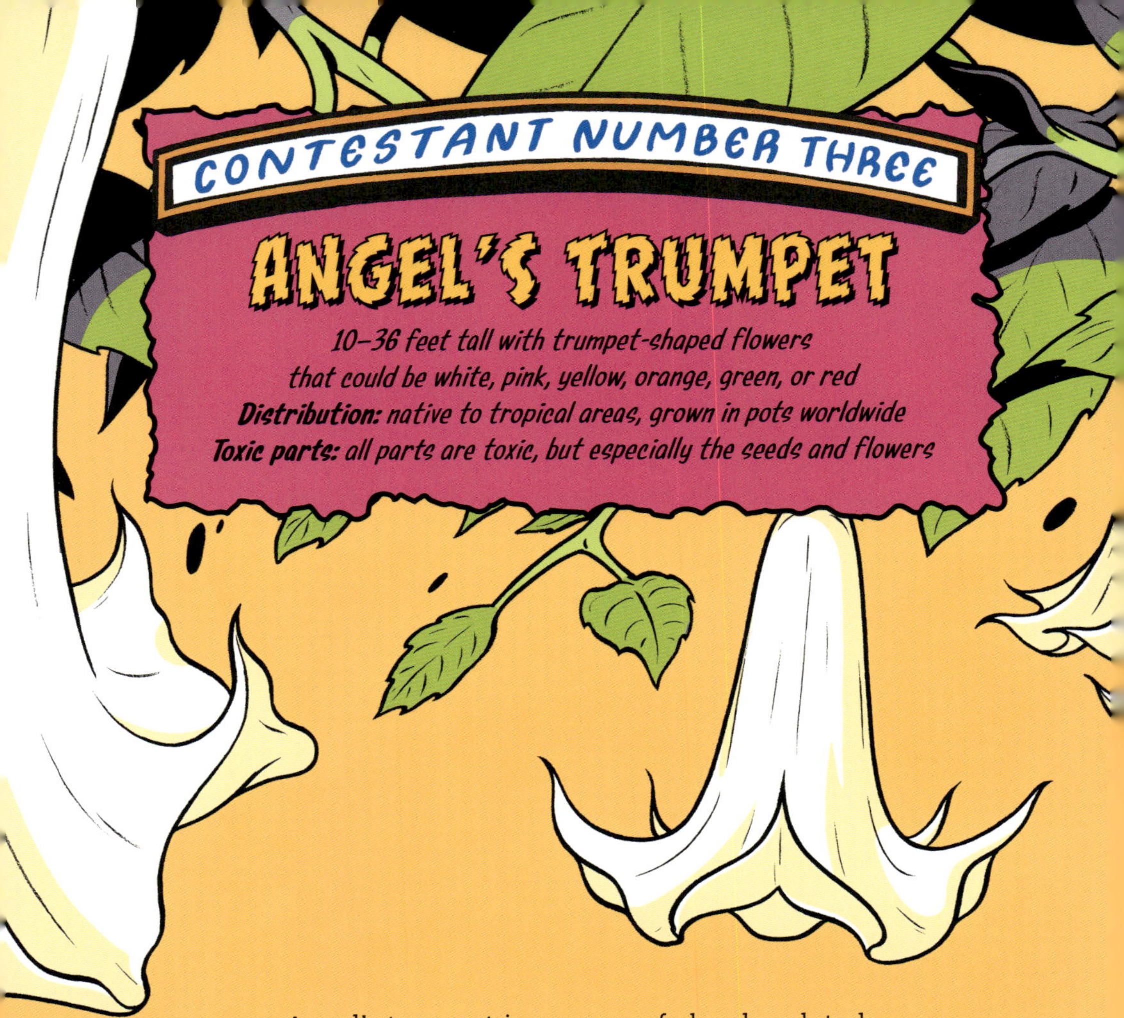

CONTESTANT NUMBER THREE

ANGEL'S TRUMPET

10–36 feet tall with trumpet-shaped flowers that could be white, pink, yellow, orange, green, or red

Distribution: *native to tropical areas, grown in pots worldwide*

Toxic parts: *all parts are toxic, but especially the seeds and flowers*

Angel's trumpet is a group of closely related flower species. They are belladonna's cousins.

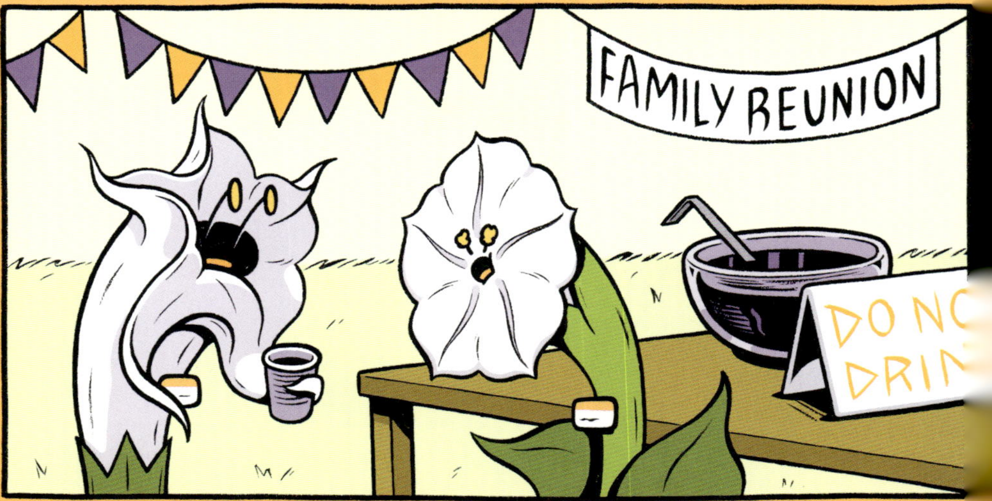
FAMILY REUNION

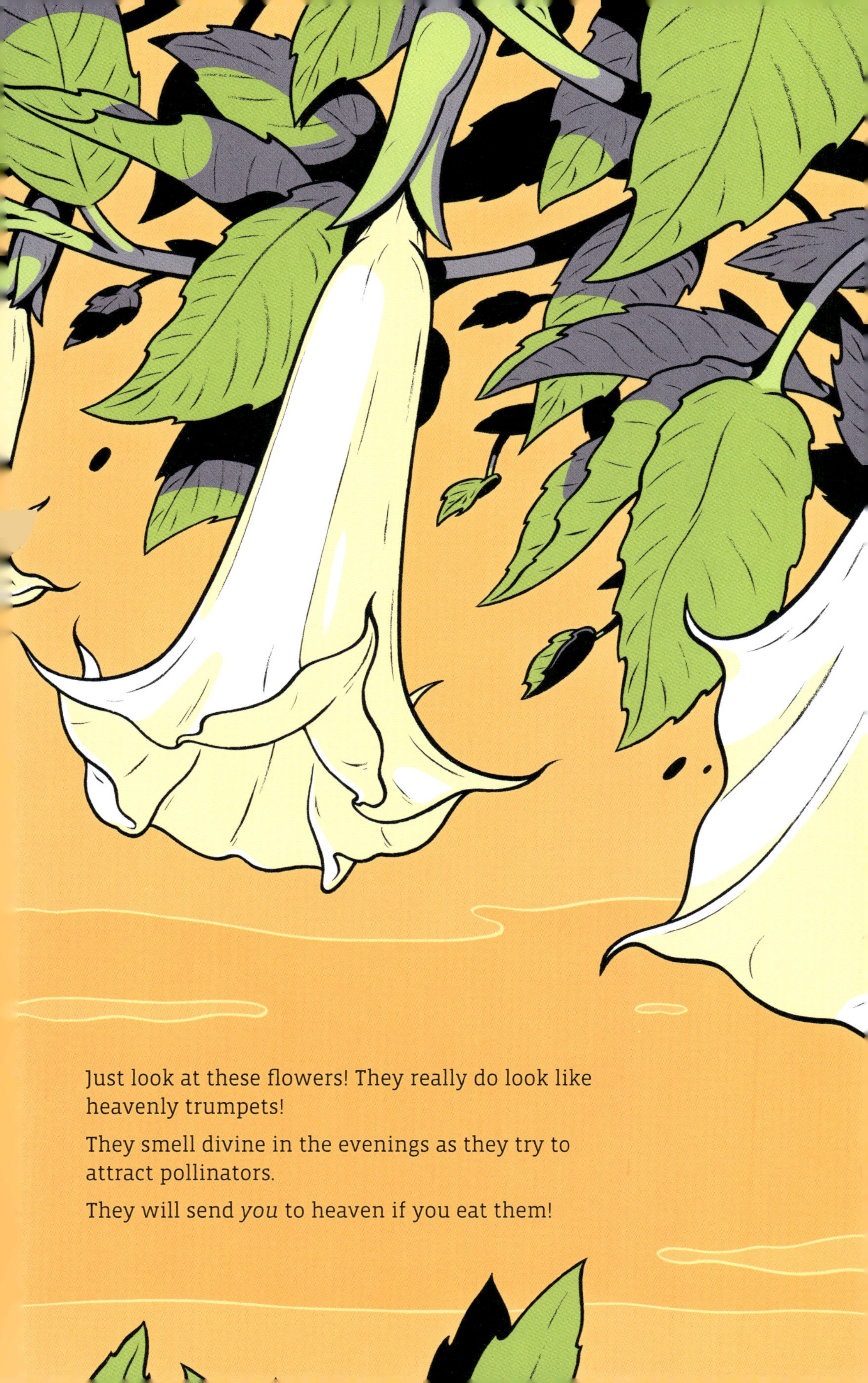

Just look at these flowers! They really do look like heavenly trumpets!

They smell divine in the evenings as they try to attract pollinators.

They will send *you* to heaven if you eat them!

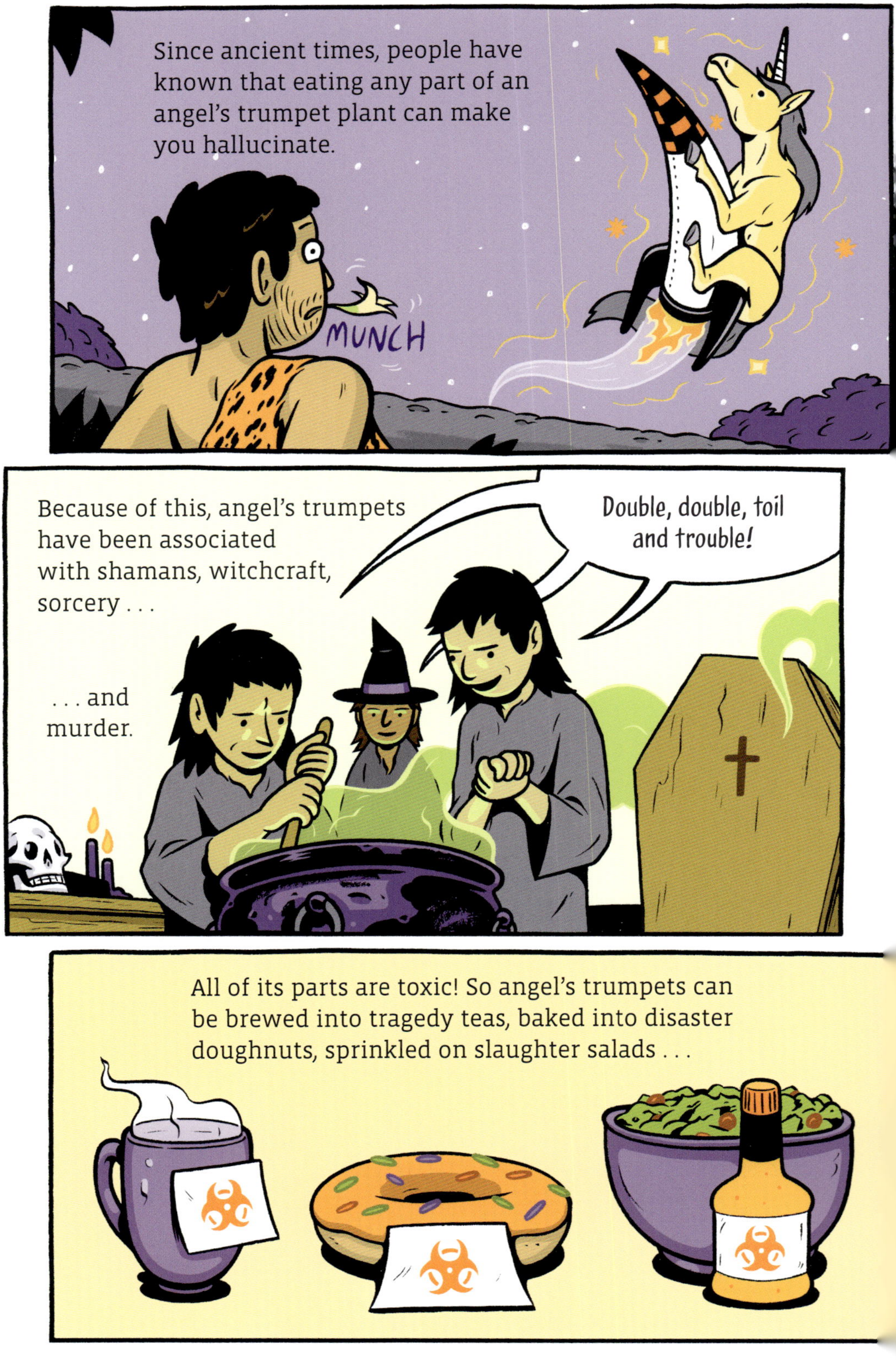
Since ancient times, people have known that eating any part of an angel's trumpet plant can make you hallucinate.
MUNCH
Because of this, angel's trumpets have been associated with shamans, witchcraft, sorcery . . .
Double, double, toil and trouble!
. . . and murder.
All of its parts are toxic! So angel's trumpets can be brewed into tragedy teas, baked into disaster doughnuts, sprinkled on slaughter salads . . .

WHAT WOULD HAPPEN IF YOU DECIDED TO SPRINKLE SOME ANGEL'S TRUMPET SEEDS ON YOUR SALAD?

Angel's trumpet has three super-toxic chemicals that attack your nervous system.

At first, your eyes will dilate unevenly. This can last for more than a day.

Meanwhile, you'll begin to hallucinate. You will hallucinate for hours. You won't be able to stop hallucinating.

Your blood pressure will go up, down, all over the place.

You'll get very hot, but you'll stop sweating.

Your mouth will become dry.

You'll begin to twitch and have seizures.

You could fall into a coma and stop breathing. That's it for you. You're done.

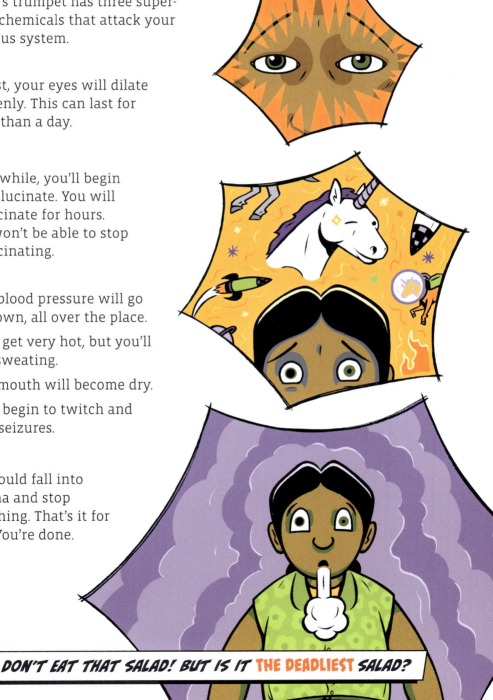

DON'T EAT THAT SALAD! BUT IS IT **THE DEADLIEST** SALAD?

CONTESTANT NUMBER FOUR

TOBACCO

3–6 feet tall
Distribution: *worldwide*
Deadly parts: *roots, stems, flowers, but especially the leaves*

Here's the only deadliest contestant that farmers grow on purpose.

Its pretty pink flowers and big, tasty leaves make it especially attractive to plenty of plant-eaters.

Tobacco wants to grow! It doesn't want to get eaten! So what does it do?

It stuffs its body with poison, of course!

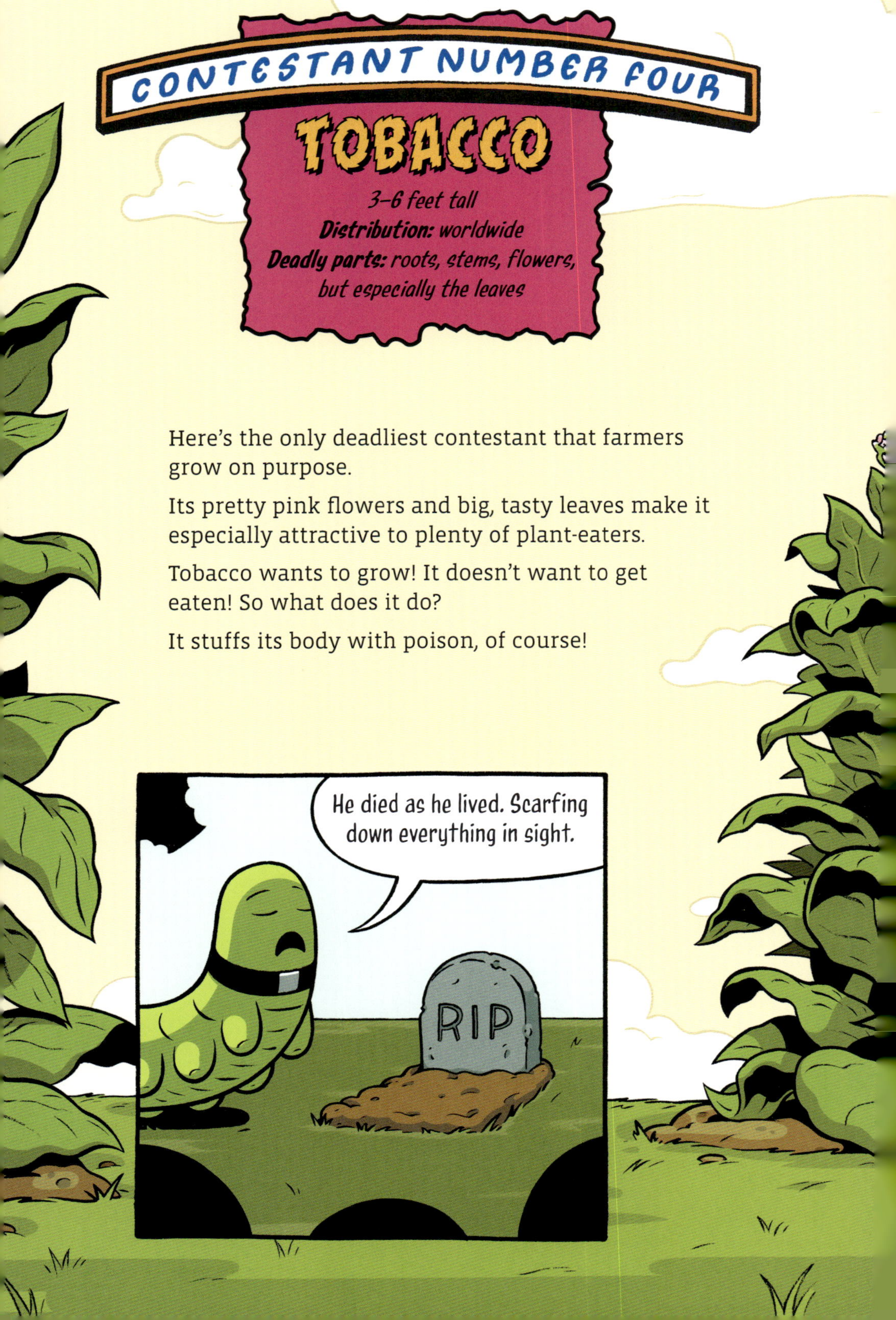
He died as he lived. Scarfing down everything in sight.
RIP

Don’t touch! People who work in tobacco fields get Green Tobacco Sickness as a result of tobacco’s toxins passing through the skin. They can get dizzy, throw up, or pass out. Tough job!

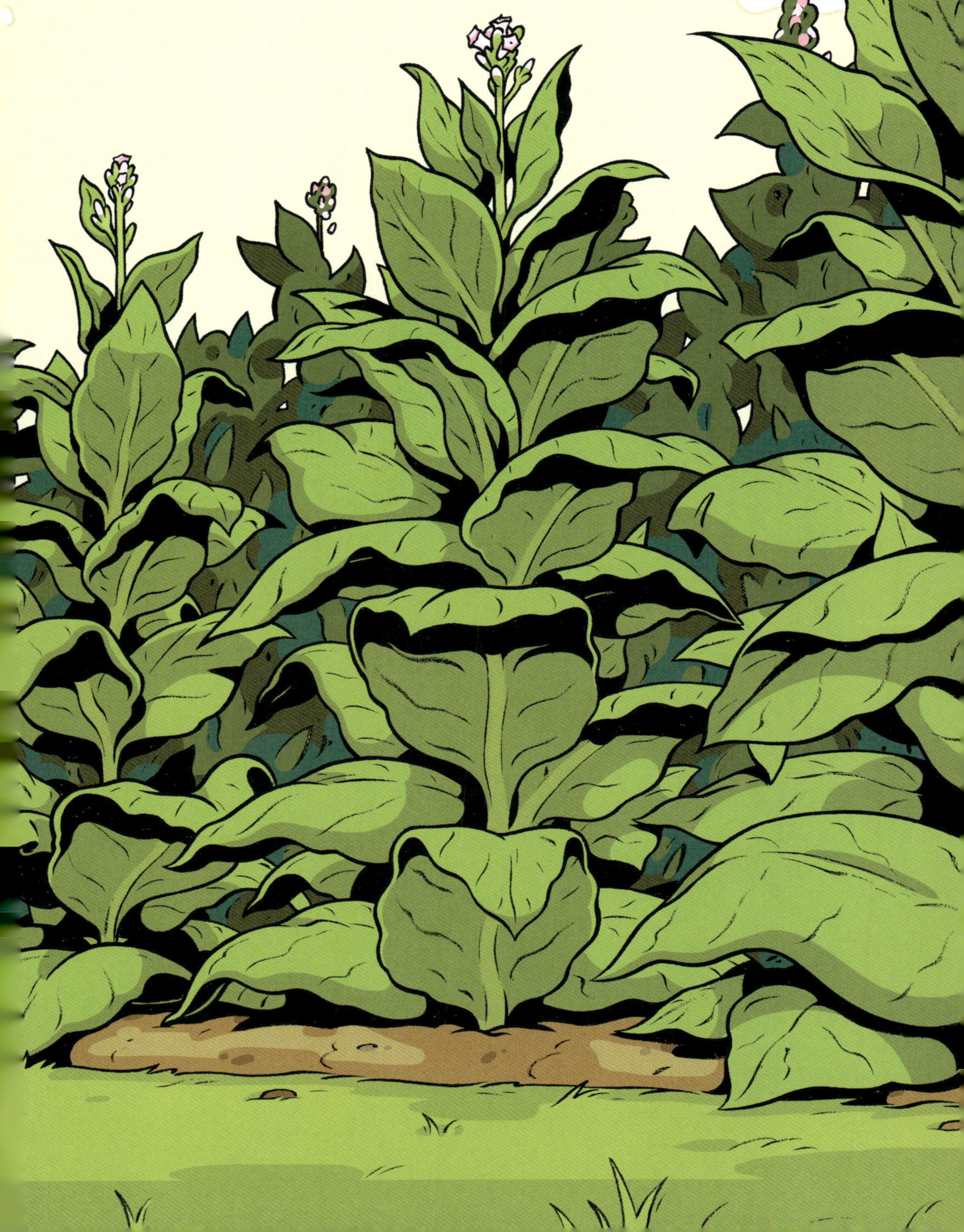

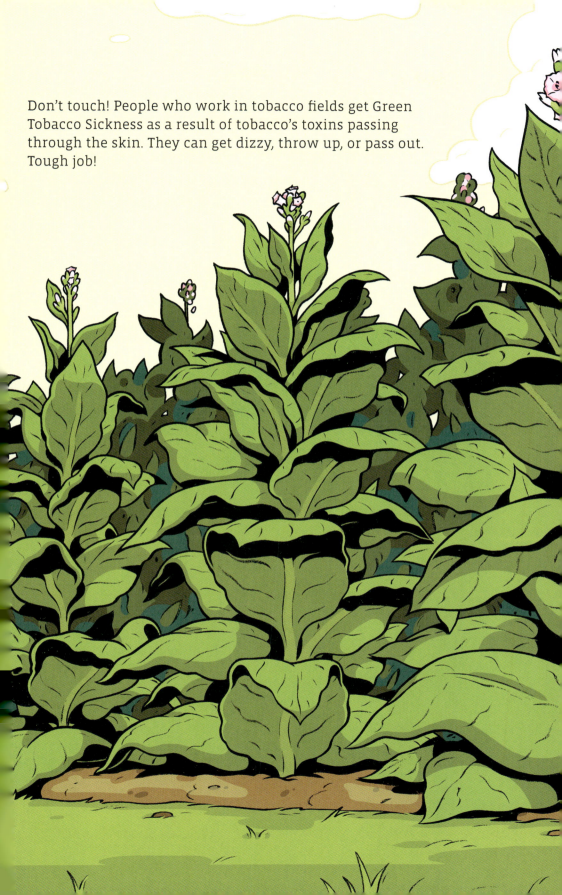

People indigenous to the Americas discovered that if they burned tobacco leaves and breathed a little in, the poison would make them feel calm and lightheaded.

When Europeans colonized America, they did what colonizers often do.

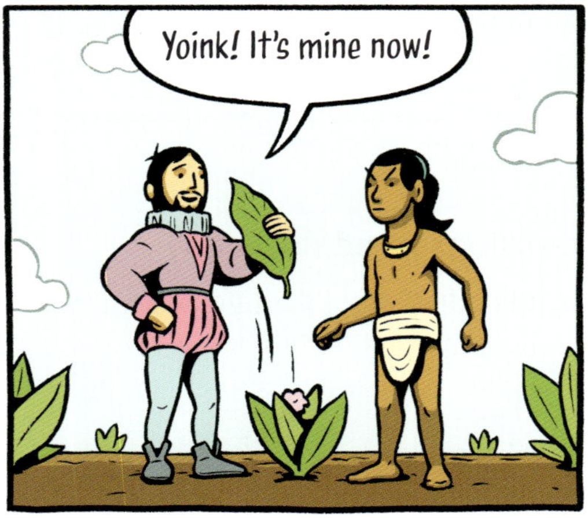
Yoink! It's mine now!

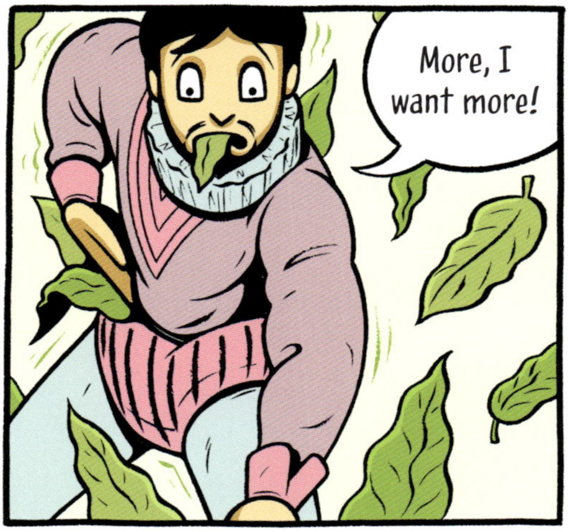
More, I want more!

They liked the way tobacco made them feel. But instead of using it every once in a while for ceremonies, they used tobacco all the time.

Pretty soon, the world was growing tobacco. People were smoking, chewing, and spitting it all over the place.

Remember, the reason people use tobacco is because of those tobacco toxins The toxins are insecticides. The defend the tobacco plant against insects.

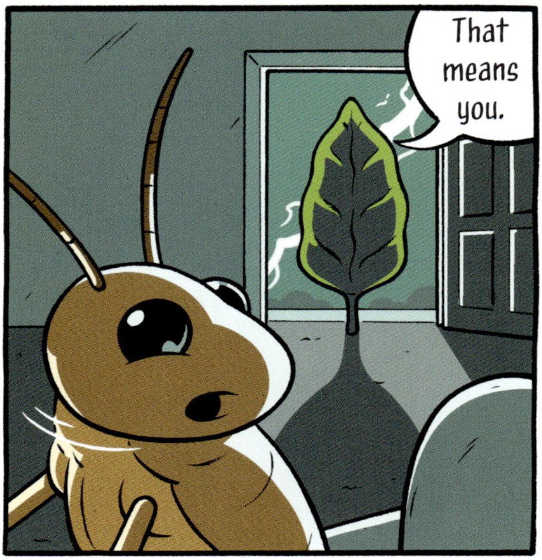
That means you.

But people put the insecticides their bodies. On purpose!

In human bodies, these insecticides go to work on people's nerves and blood vesse They speed up people's hearts.

Eating tobacco can make you sick. Smoking it can make you even sicker because smoke can permanently damage your lung

WHAT WOULD HAPPEN IF YOU DECIDED TO EAT A BUNCH OF TOBACCO PLANTS?

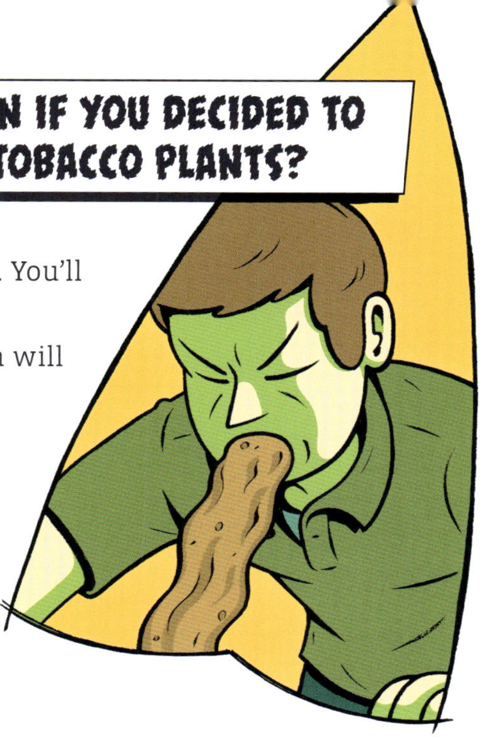

the beginning, you'll feel pretty ill. You'll art throwing up and slobbering.

ur stomach will hurt and your skin will come ghostly pale.

ur heart will race. You will breathe e you've just run a marathon.

u'll lose control of your body, ve difficulty walking, tremors, d muscle twitching.

u could have seizures.

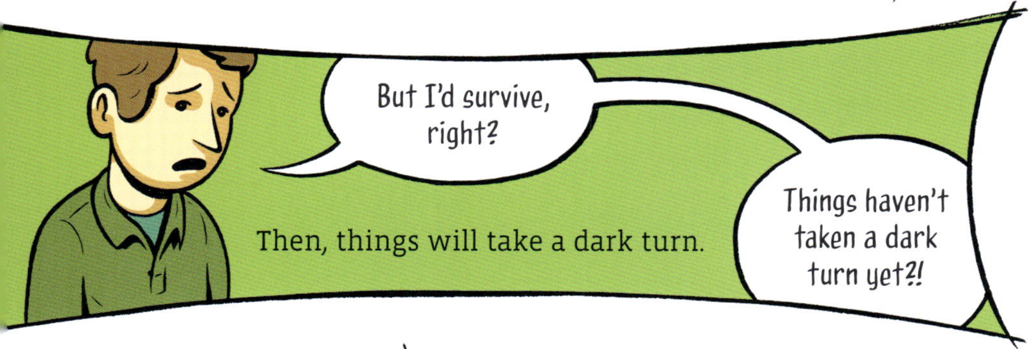
But I'd survive, right?
Then, things will take a dark turn.
Things haven't taken a dark turn yet?!

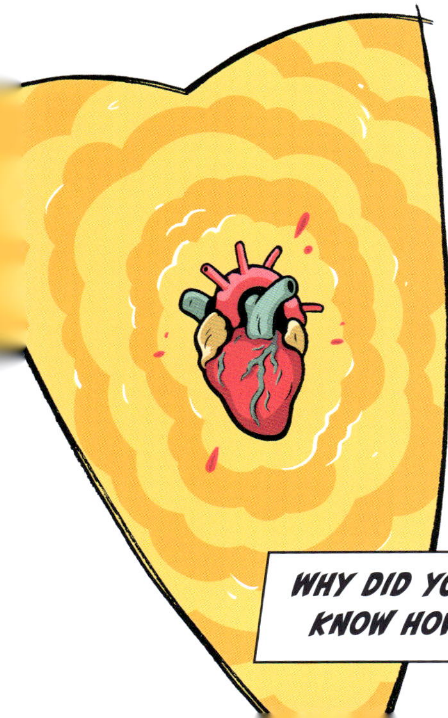

Your blood pressure will plummet. Your heart will slow down to a frighteningly quiet thump.

Your body will go into shock. You will become weak or paralyzed. You could fall into a coma.

Your breathing will become shallower until it finally stops.

WHY DID YOU EAT ALL THAT TOBACCO?! DIDN'T YOU KNOW HOW DEADLY IT WAS? IS IT THE DEADLIEST?

CONTESTANT NUMBER FIVE

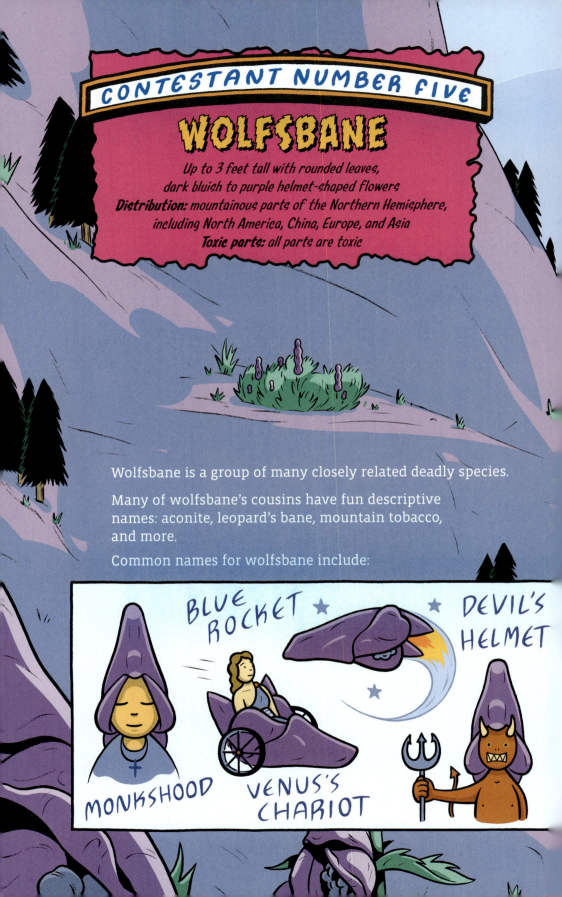

WOLFSBANE

Up to 3 feet tall with rounded leaves, dark bluish to purple helmet-shaped flowers

***Distribution:** mountainous parts of the Northern Hemisphere, including North America, China, Europe, and Asia*

***Toxic parts:** all parts are toxic*

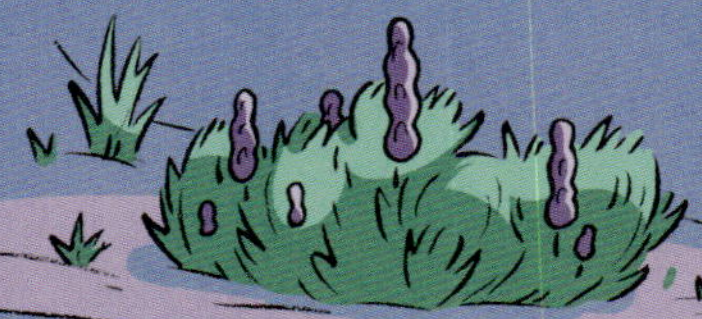

Wolfsbane is a group of many closely related deadly species.

Many of wolfsbane's cousins have fun descriptive names: aconite, leopard's bane, mountain tobacco, and more.

Common names for wolfsbane include:

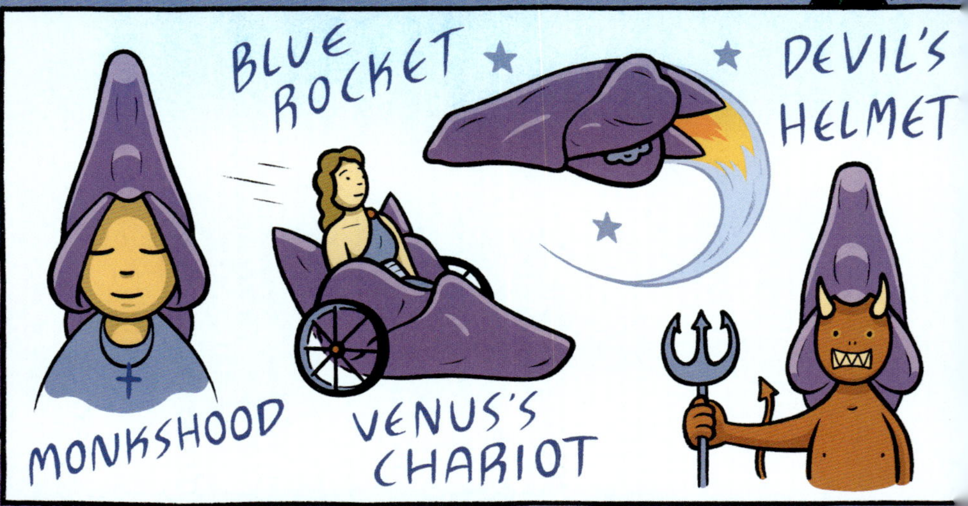
BLUE ROCKET
DEVIL'S HELMET
MONKSHOOD
VENUS'S CHARIOT

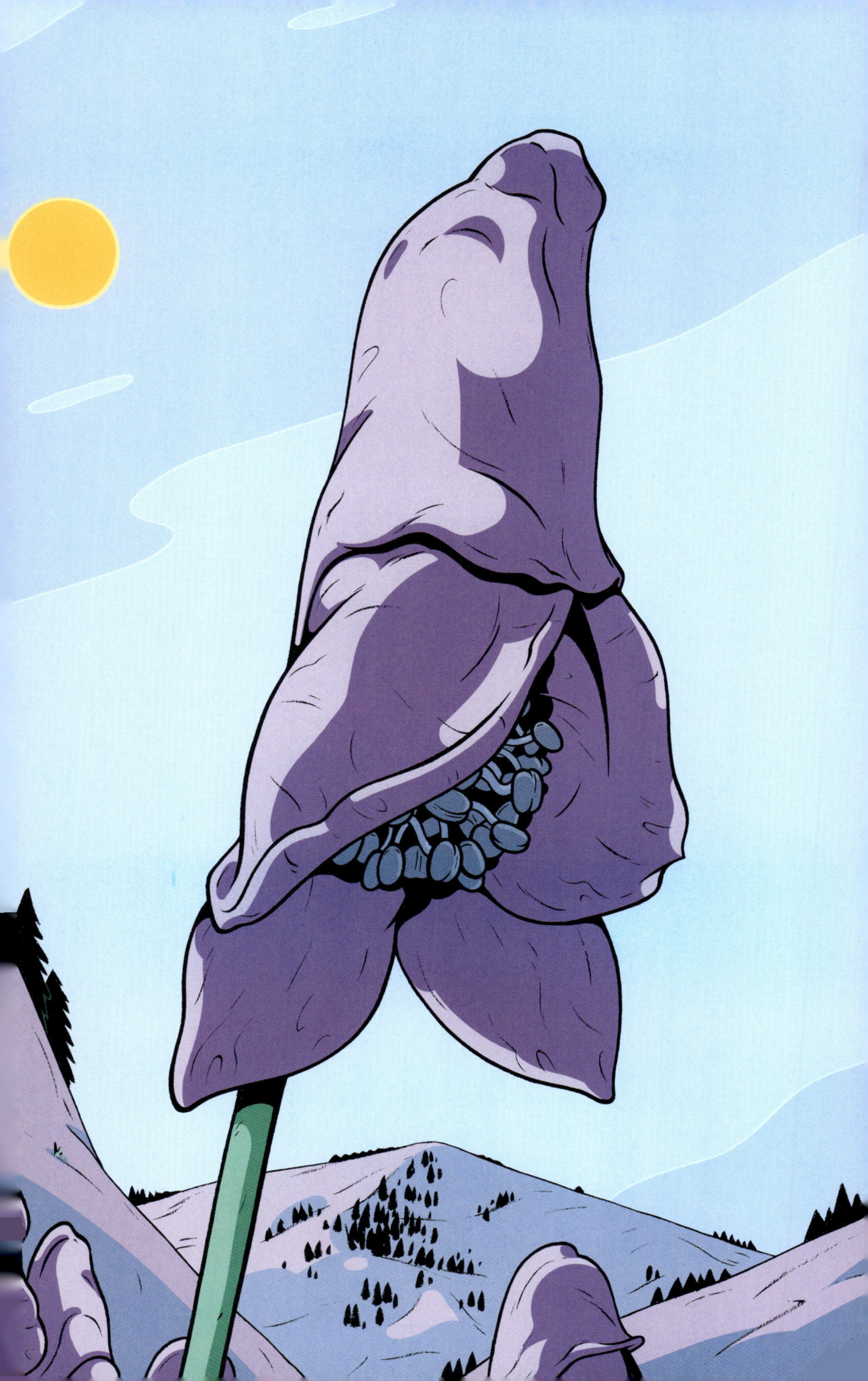

A **bane** is something that causes someone a lot of misery. Some of us (not you!) consider little siblings to be banes.

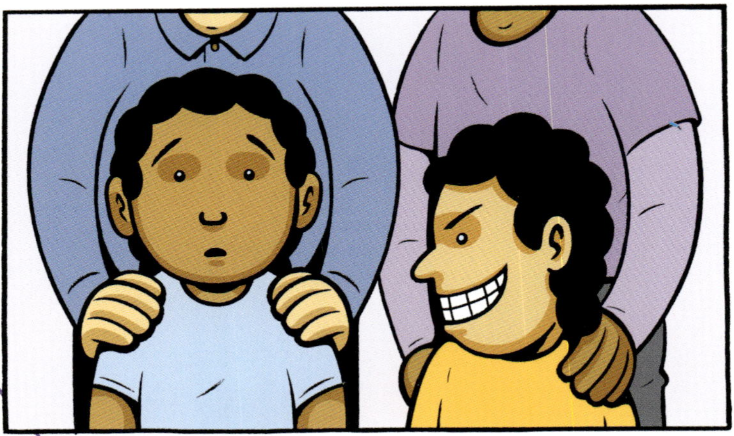

In ancient times wolfsbane caused wolves a lot of misery. People dipped their arrow tips in a mixture made from the deadly plant before they went hunting for wolves.

The wolves hardly stood a chance.

You would also hardly stand a chance.

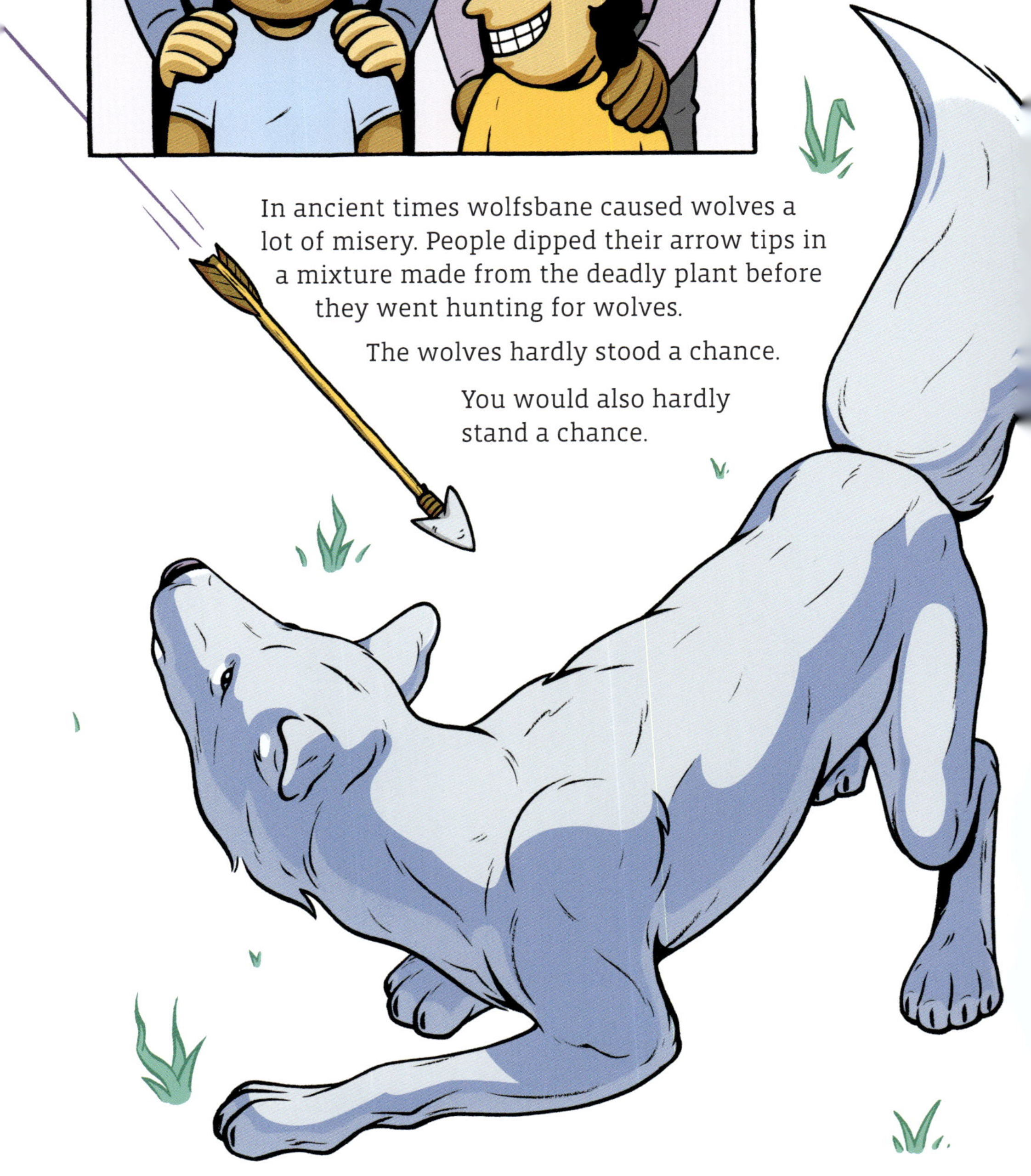

WHAT IF SOMEONE ACCIDENTALLY SHOT YOU WITH A WOLFSBANE-LACED ARROW?

If the arrow doesn't kill you, in about an hour you'll start to feel sick to your stomach.

Then, you'll start to feel like your mouth and face are burning.

You'll tingle and feel numb.

Your abdomen will burn like your mouth.

Your heart rate will slow, your blood pressure will drop, and you'll get confused, start to sweat, feel dizzy, and have trouble breathing.

No known antidote exists. If your body can't get rid of the poison, you'll die.

ARROWS NEEDED:

You can get the poison wolfsbane into your system through your skin by simply brushing against the plants.

If you somehow got a whole lot of wolfsbane into your system, your heart would stop instantly. It would look as if someone strangled you.

This is why wolfsbane extract was a useful murder method before blood could be tested for toxins.

No one was in the room. But he was strangled!

THAT'S COLD. BUT IS IT THE DEADLIEST?

CONTESTANT NUMBER SIX

POISON HEMLOCK

Up to 3 feet tall, smooth, hollow, purple-spotted stems with loose clusters of small, white, five-petaled flowers

Distribution: *native to Europe and North Africa, now found in North and South America and parts of Asia, Australia, and New Zealand*

Toxic parts: *all parts are toxic, but especially the seeds and roots*

Hemlock is a word for a kind of tree. They often grow along rivers, where they help stabilize the river banks and maintain the soil.

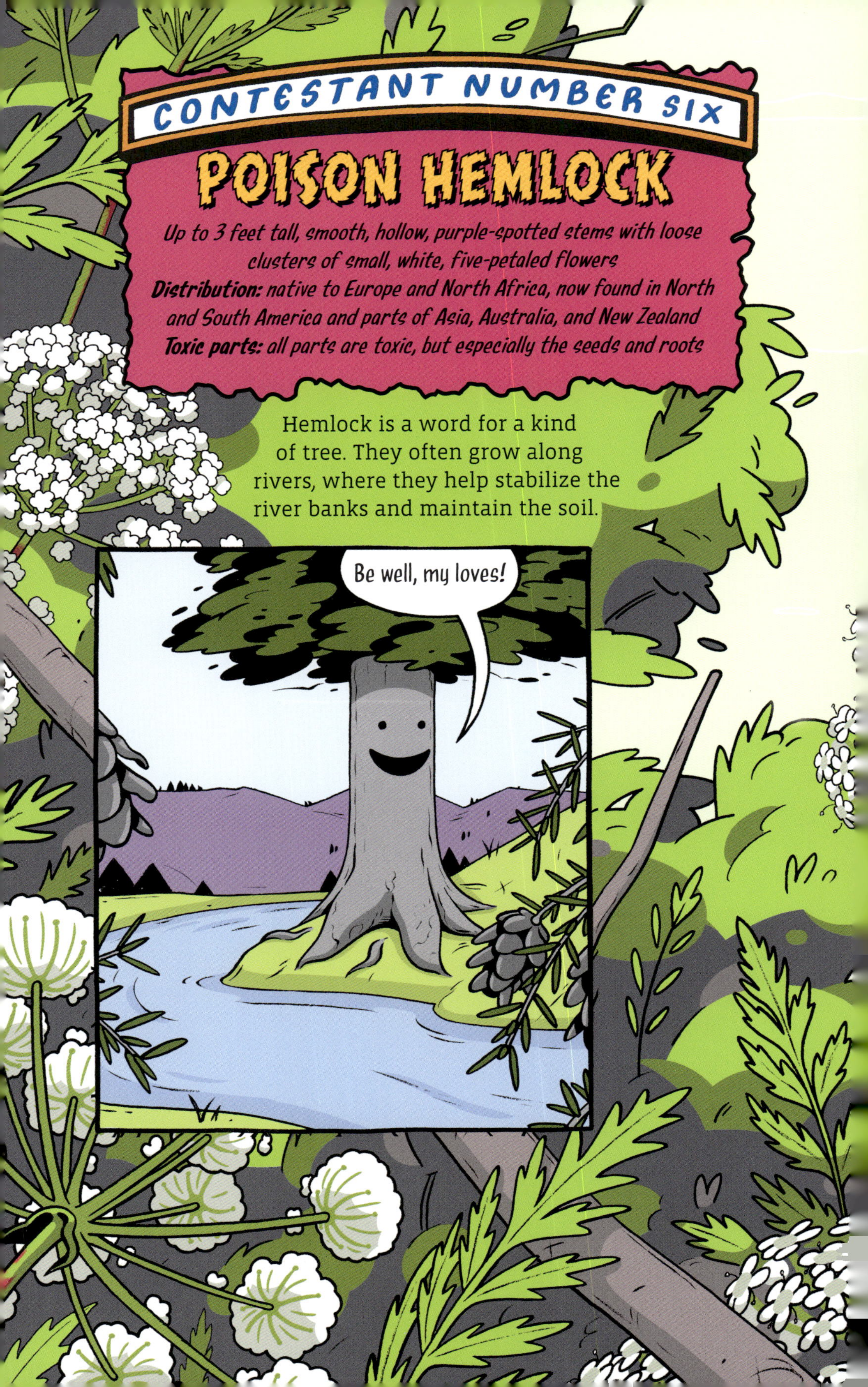
Be well, my loves!

Hemlock is also a word for a type of flower that can make you pretty sick.

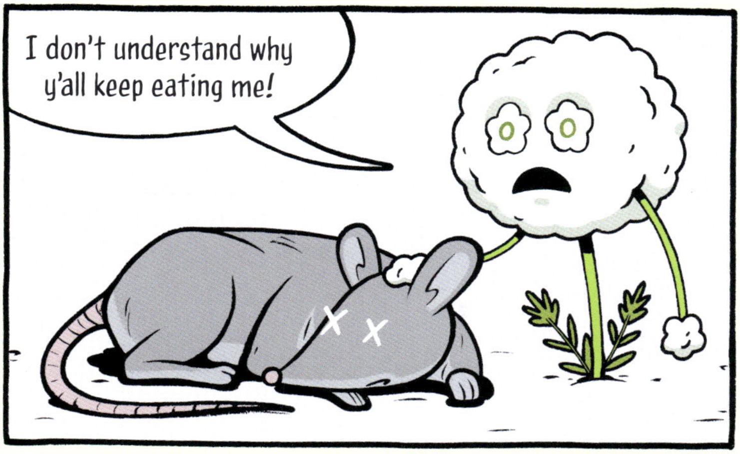
I don't understand why y'all keep eating me!

A hemlock flower looks like a lot of other types of flowers.

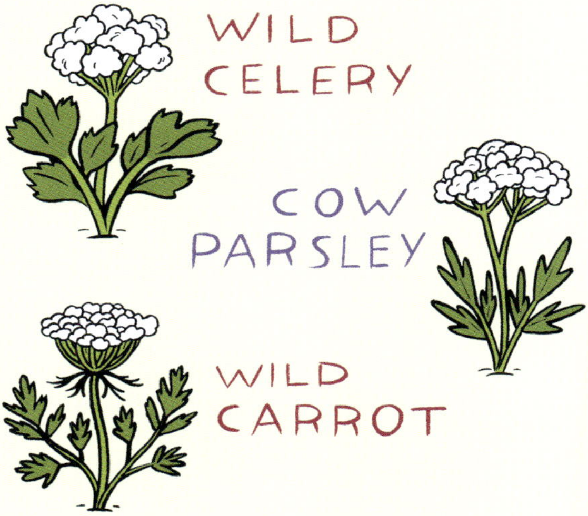
WILD CELERY
COW PARSLEY
WILD CARROT

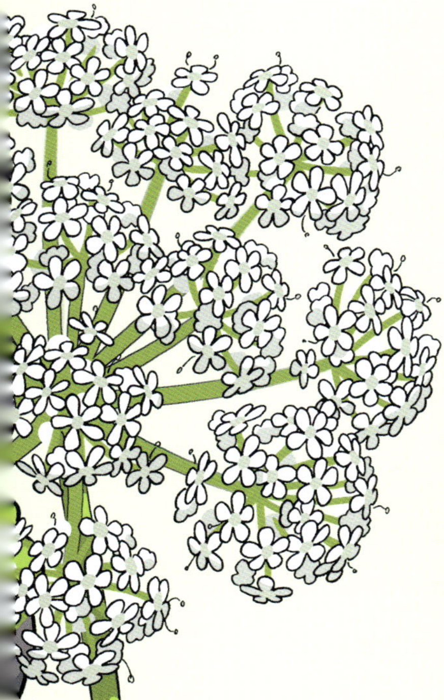

It's much deadlier.

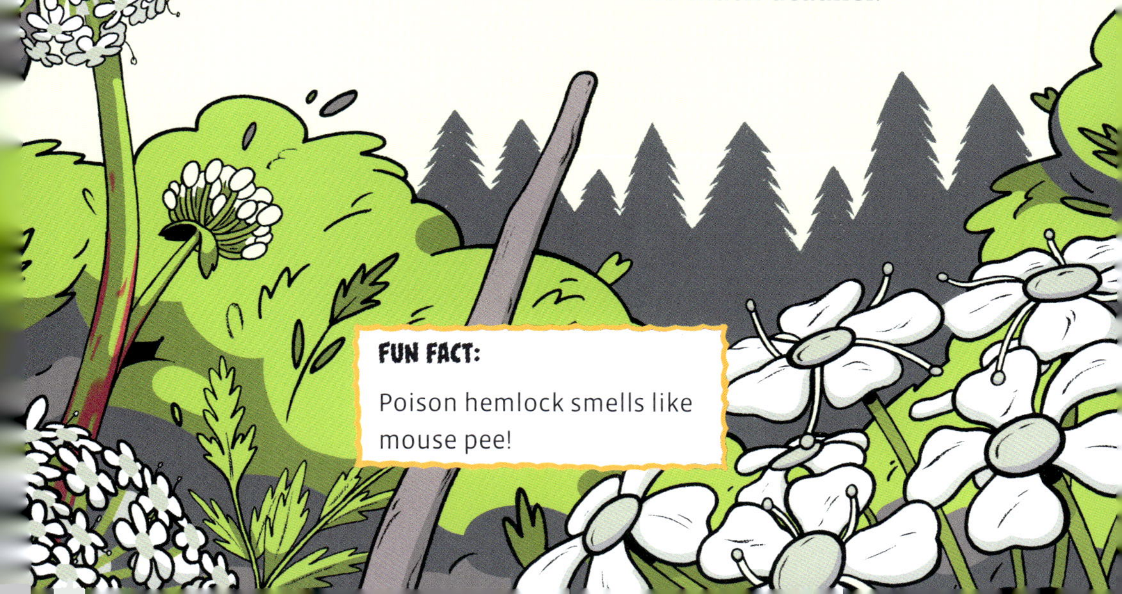

FUN FACT:

Poison hemlock smells like mouse pee!

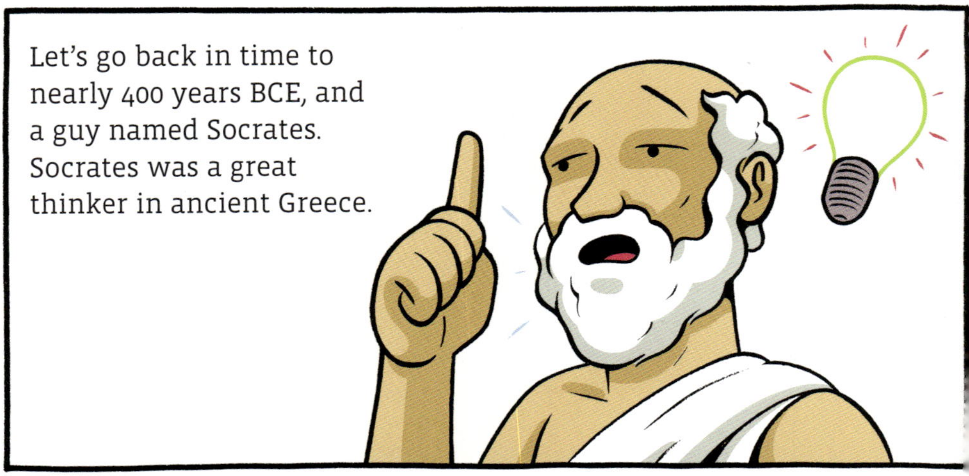
Let's go back in time to nearly 400 years BCE, and a guy named Socrates. Socrates was a great thinker in ancient Greece.

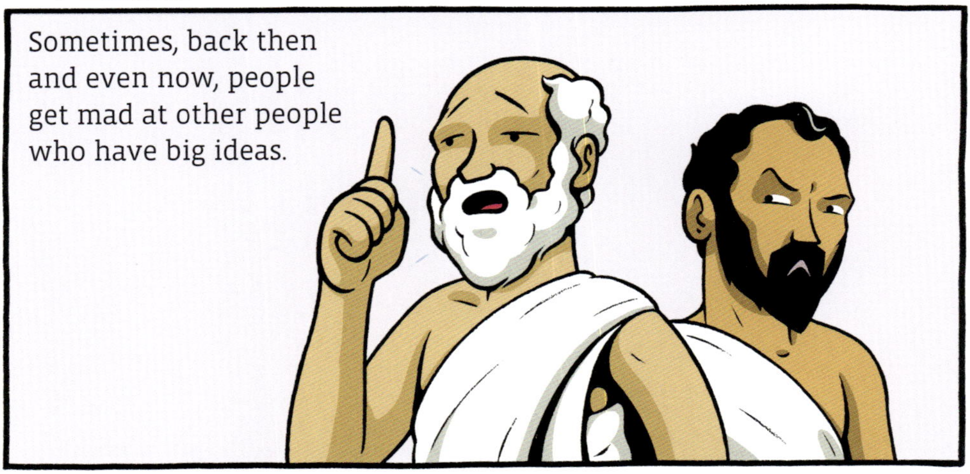
Sometimes, back then and even now, people get mad at other people who have big ideas.

For Socrates's big ideas, the government sentenced him to death.

Socrates knew he had no way out, so he agreed to his death sentence.

He drank a mug of hemlock poison.

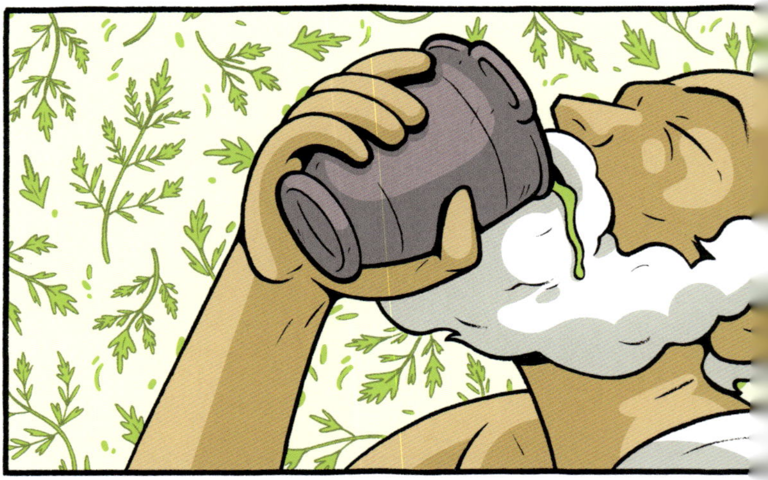

WHAT IF YOU WERE SOCRATES? WHAT WOULD HAPPEN TO YOU AFTER YOU DRANK THE POISON?

Poison hemlock has more than five toxins that act on your **central nervous system**.

CENTRAL NERVOUS SYSTEM: the parts of your body, including your brain and spinal cord, that control how you think, move around, and feel.

Within fifteen minutes of drinking your hemlock cocktail, your muscles will feel weak. You'll lose control of your arms and legs.

You will throw up as your body tries to get the poison out, but it's too late.

You'll tremble and stagger, and your pulse will go from barely beating to racing.

You'll slobber but you won't be able to chew.

You'll slip into a coma and become unable to breathe. This will kill you.

lesson: Keep having big ideas. Don't drink the poison. It can kill you.

BUT IS THIS ENOUGH TO BE THE DEADLIEST POISON? IT'S TIME TO FIND OUT!

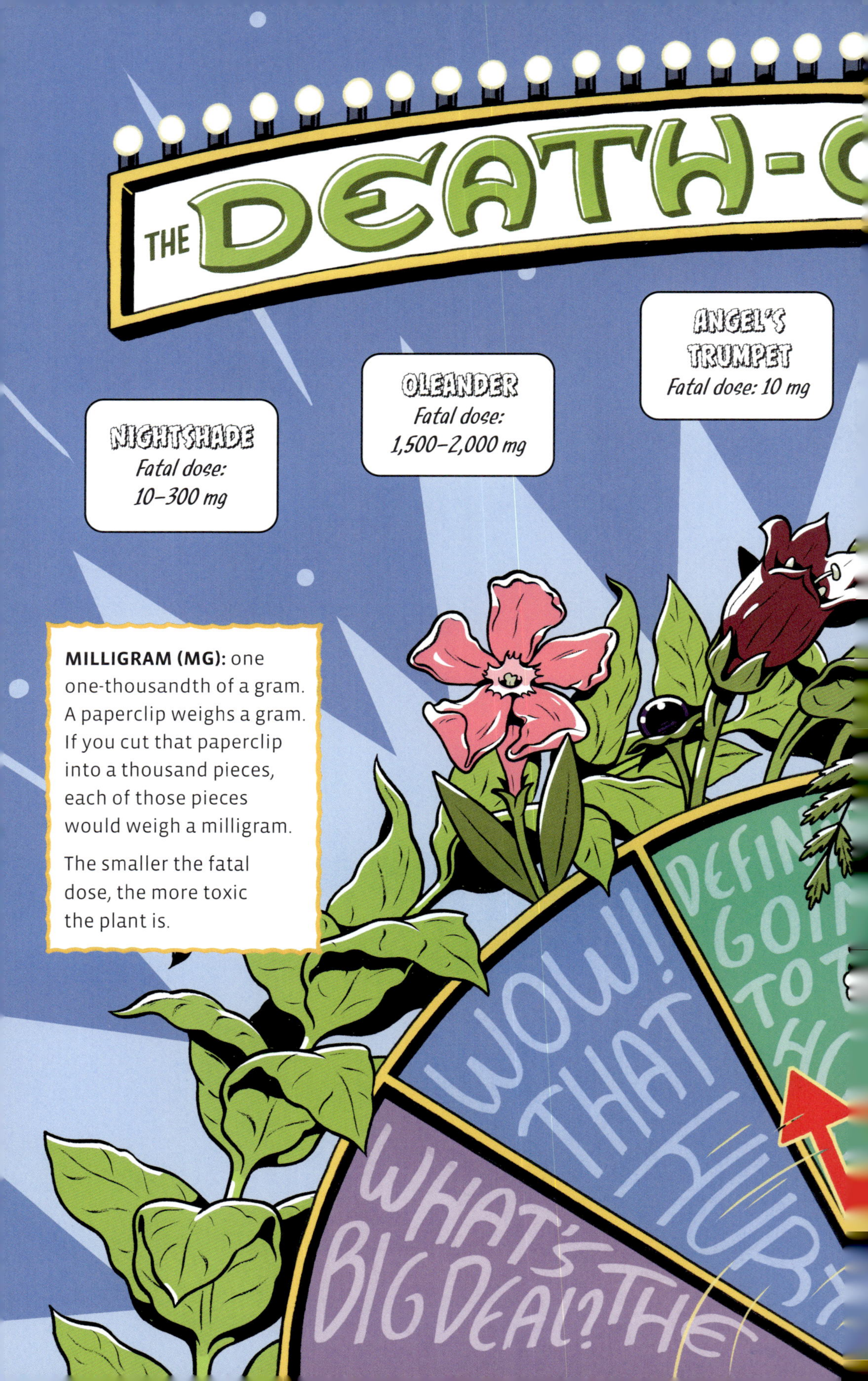
THE DEATH-
ANGEL'S TRUMPET
Fatal dose: 10 mg
OLEANDER
Fatal dose: 1,500–2,000 mg
NIGHTSHADE
Fatal dose: 10–300 mg
WOW! THAT
WHAT'S
BIG DEAL? THE

MILLIGRAM (MG): one one-thousandth of a gram. A paperclip weighs a gram. If you cut that paperclip into a thousand pieces, each of those pieces would weigh a milligram.

The smaller the fatal dose, the more toxic the plant is.

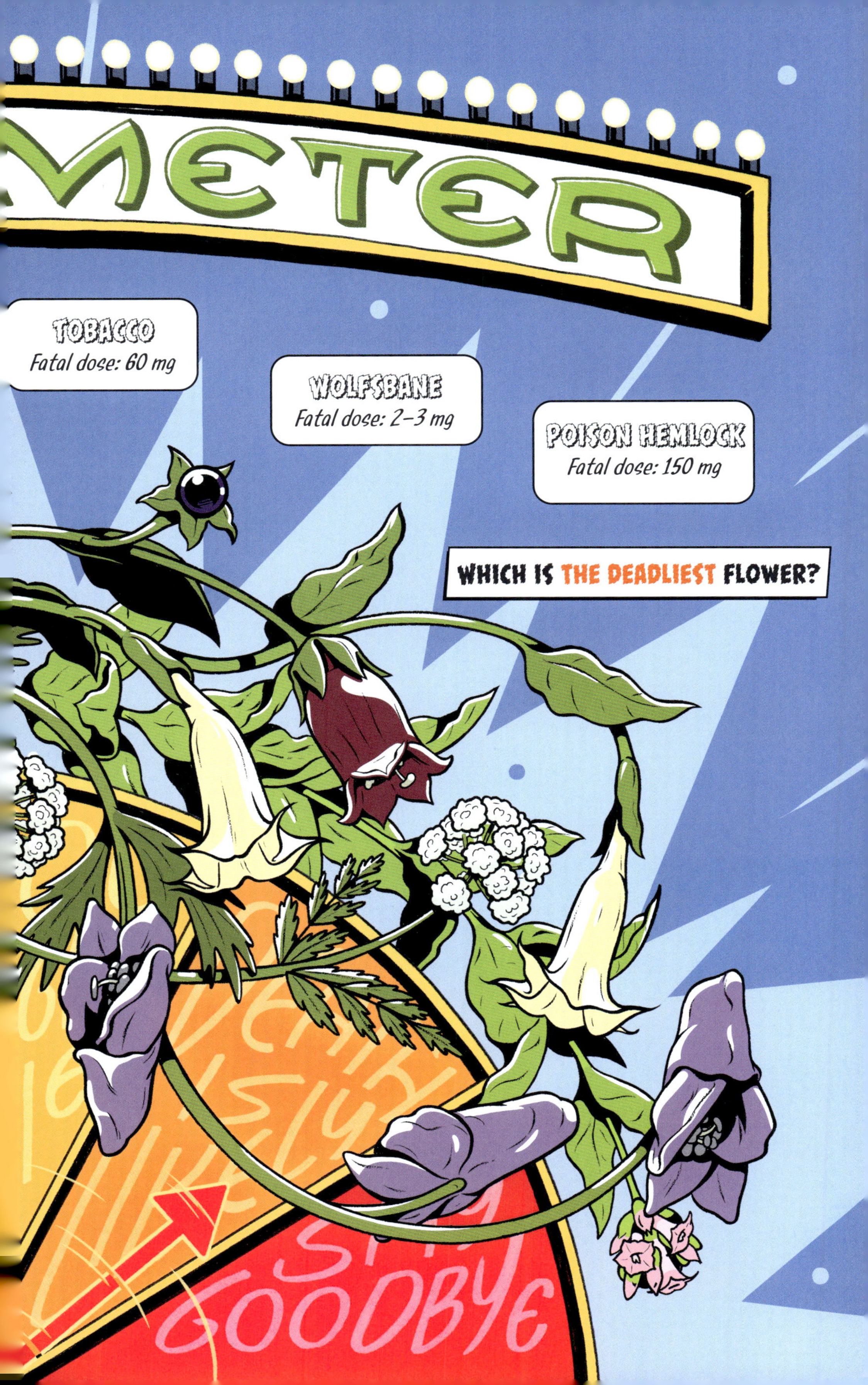
METER
TOBACCO
Fatal dose: 60 mg
WOLFSBANE
Fatal dose: 2–3 mg
POISON HEMLOCK
Fatal dose: 150 mg
WHICH IS THE DEADLIEST FLOWER?
GOODBYE

IN THIS BATTLE OF THE BEAUTIES, THE DEADLIEST FLOWERING PLANT IS . . .

. . . NOT WOLFSBANE!

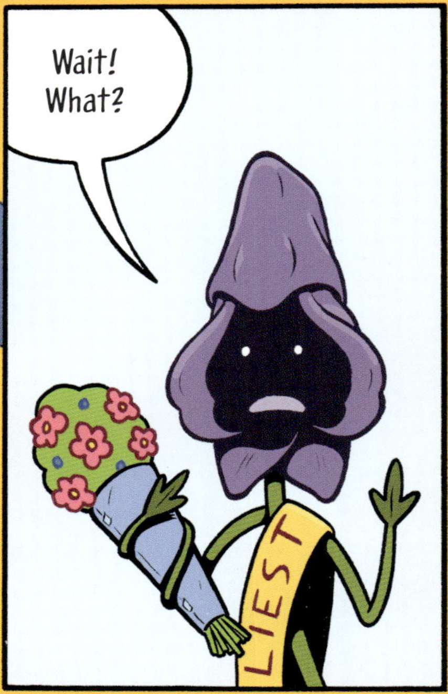

Wait! What?
LIEST

Wolfsbane is the most toxic of these plants. It would surely eliminate you in no time flat if you ate it.

But people don't eat wolfsbane very often.

In fact, fewer than ten deaths a year are attributed to wolfsbane poisoning.

THE DEADLIEST IS . . .

TOBACCO!

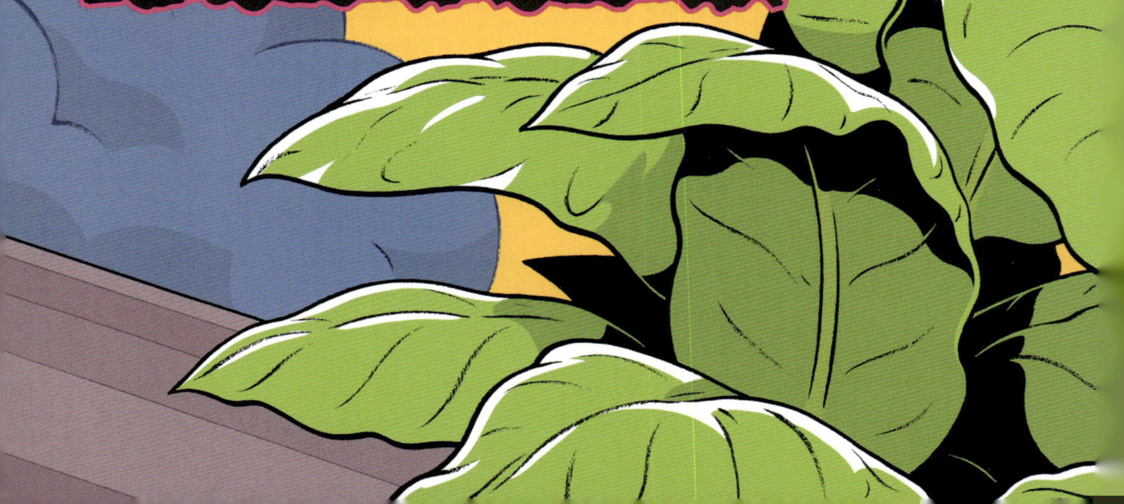

Lots of people put tobacco in their bodies on purpose. Tobacco is addictive. And the way people most commonly put it in their bodies, by smoking it, can wear their bodies down in all sorts of ways.

The World Health Organization estimates that tobacco kills about 8 million people each year.

That's compared to:

Less than one death a year, on average, from nightshade poisoning . . .

Less than one death, on average, from oleander poisoning . . .

Less than one to ten deaths, on average, from angel's trumpet poisoning . . .

Less than one to ten deaths, on average, from wolfsbane . . .

And less than one death, on average, from poison hemlock.

REMEMBER!

These are six of the deadliest plants on the planet, but they're not the only dangerous or deadly plants.

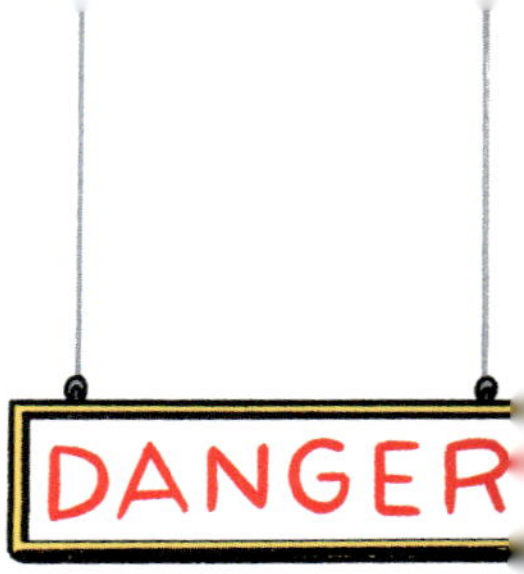
DANGER

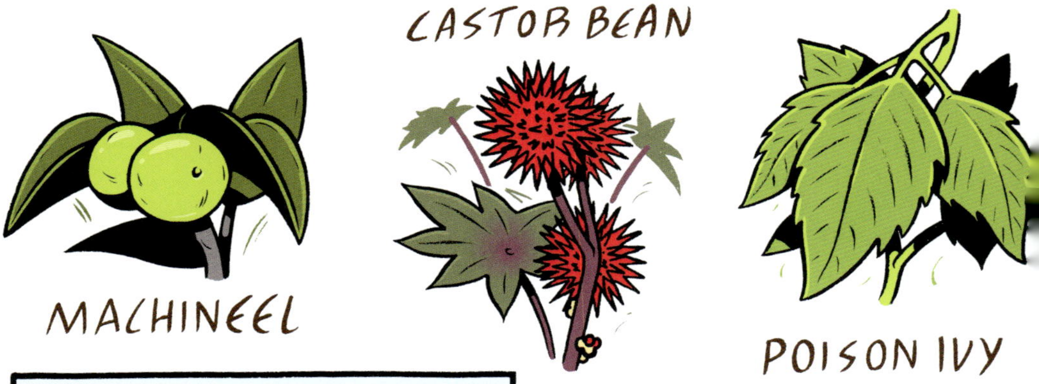
CASTOR BEAN
MACHINEEL
POISON IVY

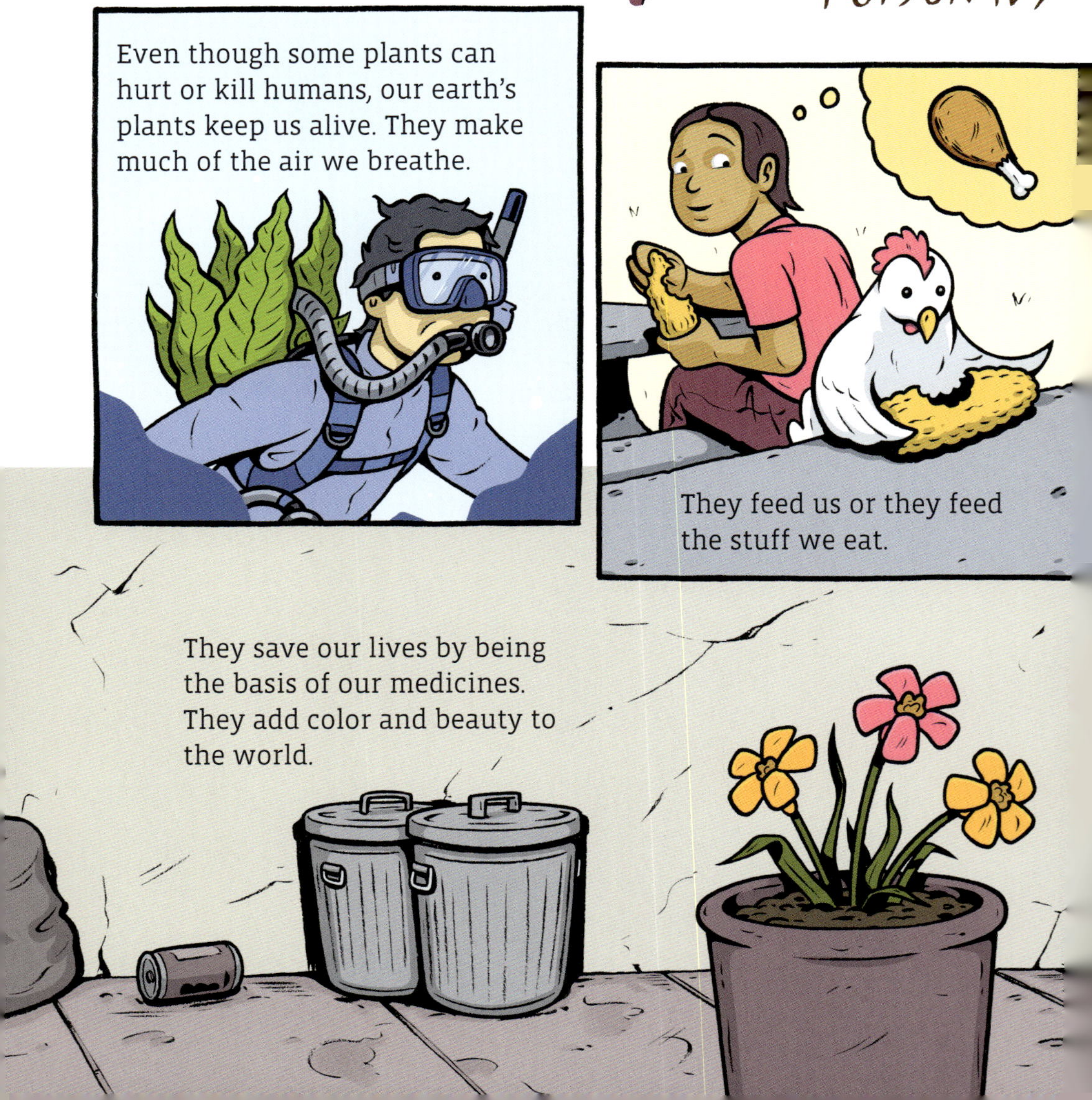
Even though some plants can hurt or kill humans, our earth's plants keep us alive. They make much of the air we breathe.
They feed us or they feed the stuff we eat.
They save our lives by being the basis of our medicines. They add color and beauty to the world.

WHAT CAN WE DO WITH PLANTS?

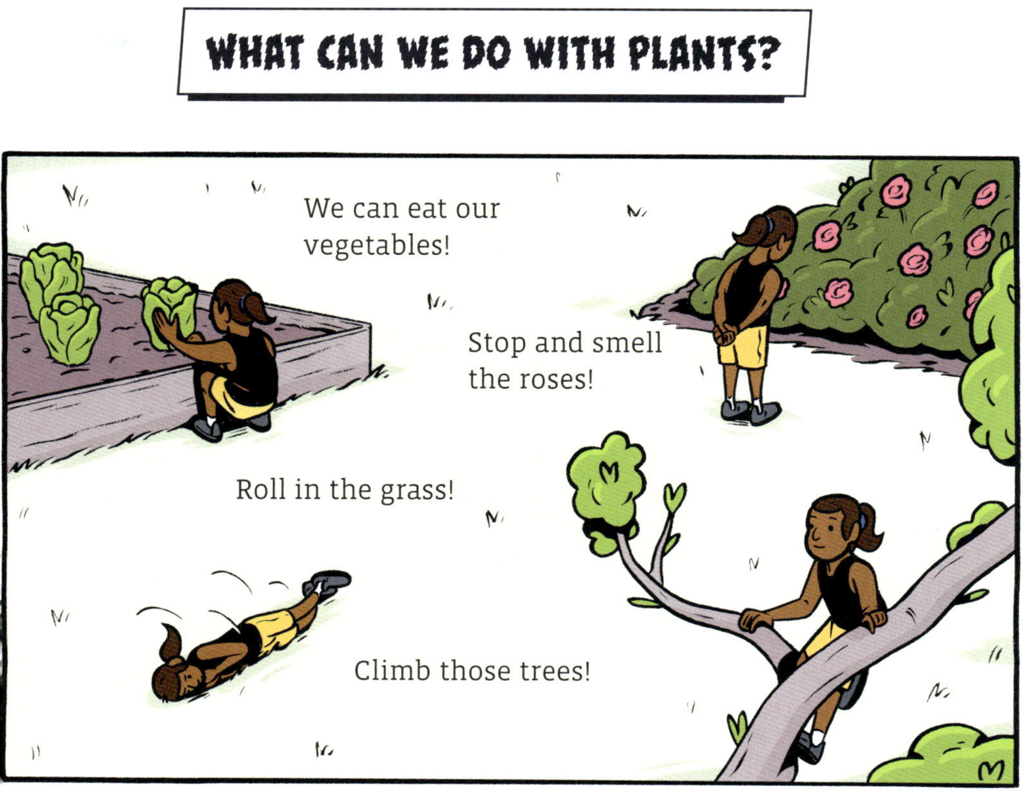
We can eat our vegetables!
Stop and smell the roses!
Roll in the grass!
Climb those trees!

Just don’t pick (or eat!) the plants you don’t know. Enjoy them from a distance, and marvel at how colorful (and amazing) our natural world really is.

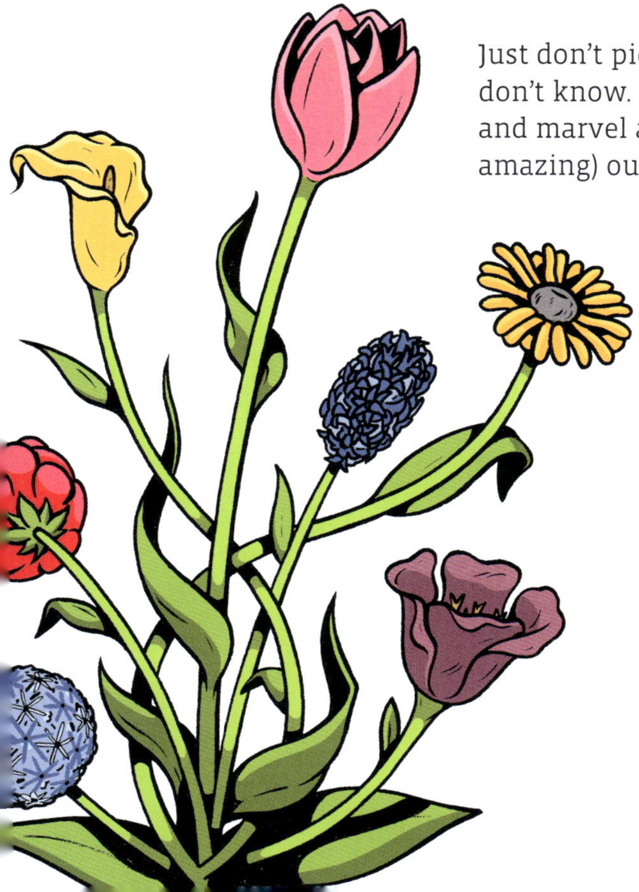

WE NEED THEM! LET’S LOVE THEM!

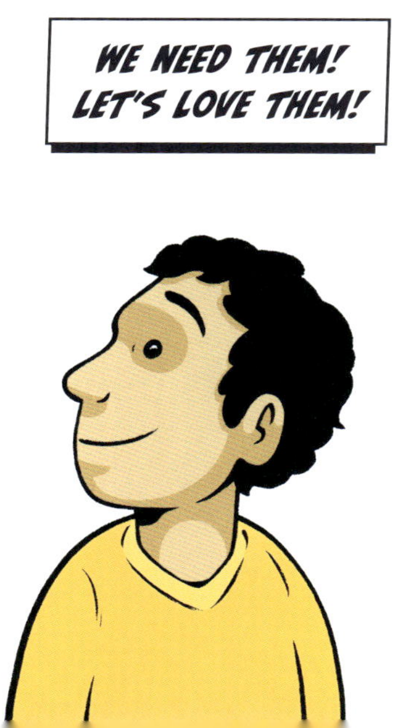

ULTIMATE DEADLY!

Each of these deadly flowers has its own superpowers. Combine them to create your own Ultimate Deadly creature! Use these superpowers we found, or discover more and use those!

BELLADONNA

Superpower:

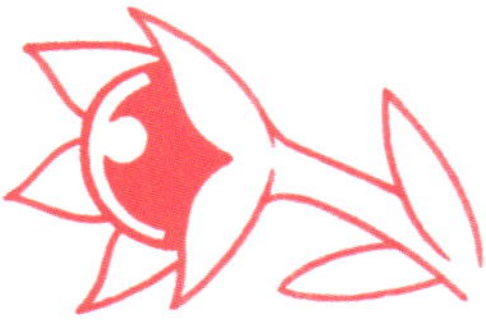

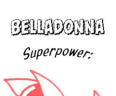

Tasty-looking berries

OLEANDER

Superpower:

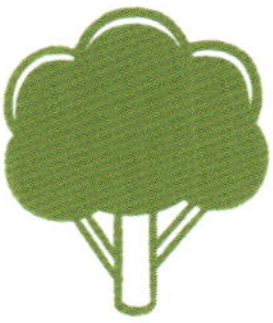

A nice, bushy tree

ANGEL'S TRUMPE

Superpower:

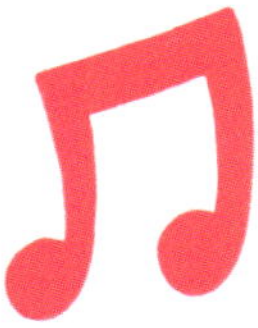

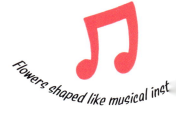

Flowers shaped like musical inst

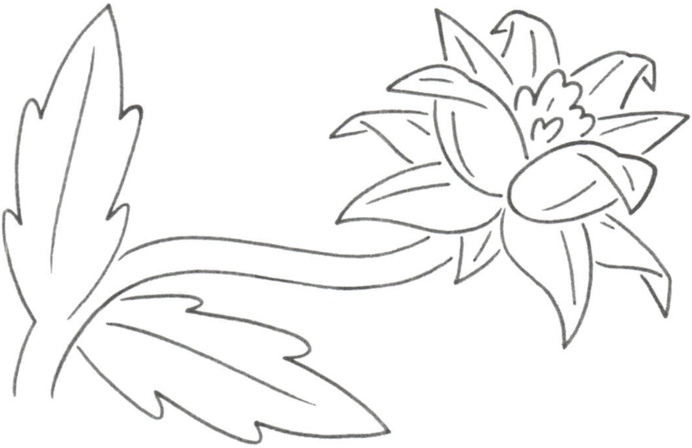

TOBACCO

Superpower:

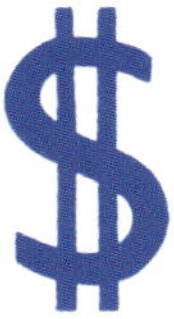

Sold in stores

WOLFSBANE

Superpower:

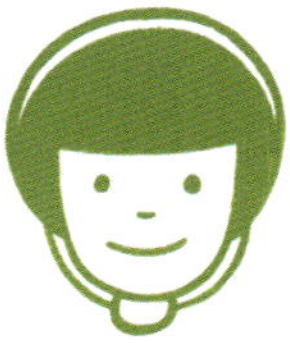

Helmet-shaped flowers

POISON HEMLOC

Superpower:

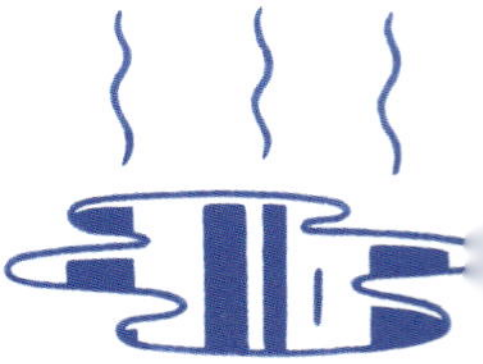

Smells like mouse pe

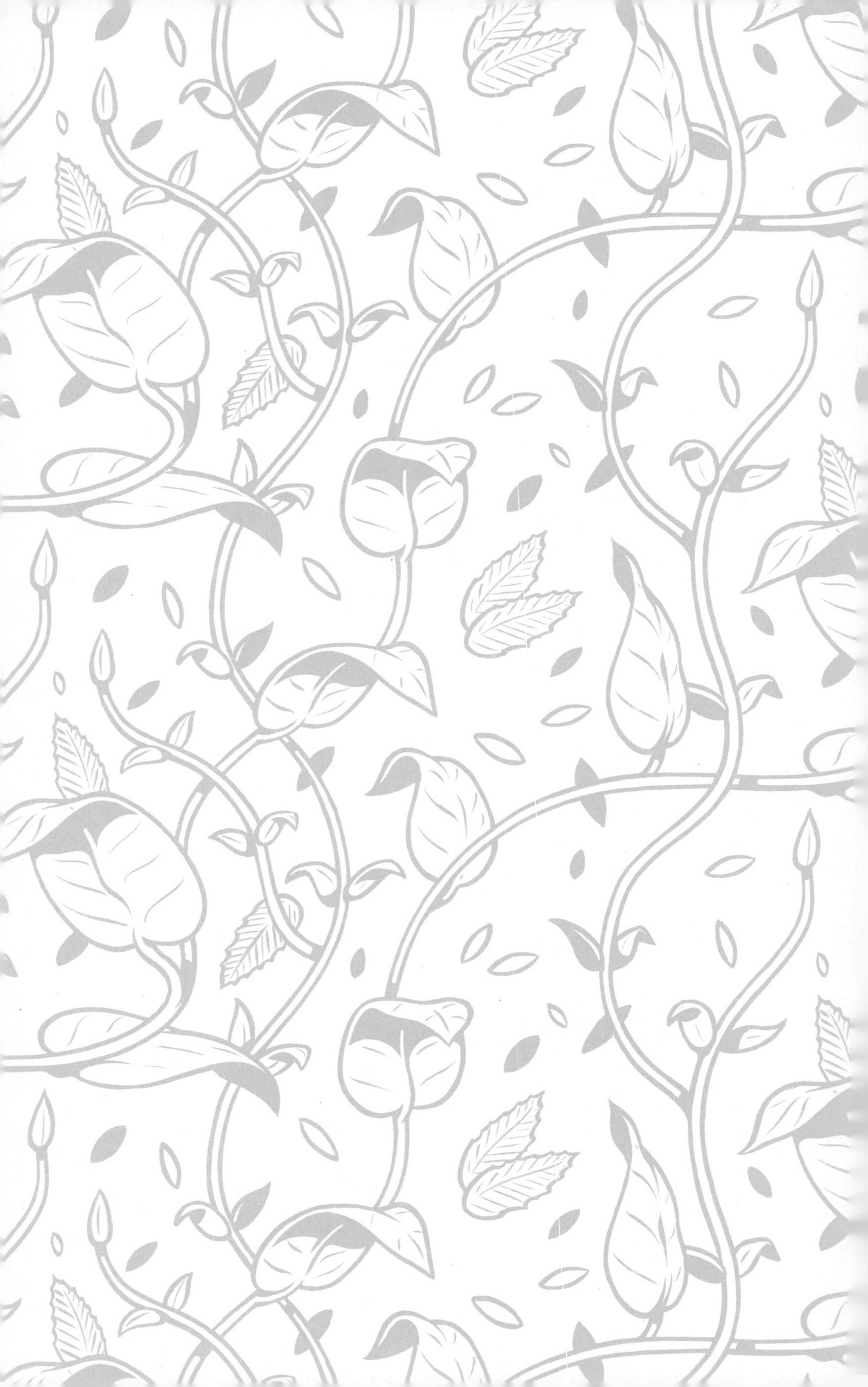